TT
880
.V33

Vane, Peter K.

Pebble people, pets
& things

DATE			

PEBBLE
PEOPLE,
PETS
&
THINGS

Pebble People, Pets & Things

PETER K. VANE

BUTTERICK PUBLISHING

Book design by Ron Shey
Color photographs by Edward Scibetta
Black and white photographs by Peter K. Vane
Illustrations by Mel Klapholtz
Library of Congress Catalog Card Number: 77-89711
International Standard Book Number: 0-88421-038-3
Copyright © 1977 by Butterick Publishing
161 Sixth Avenue
New York, New York 10013
A Division of American Can Company

CONTENTS

INTRODUCTION

If you are looking for a natural art form—an inexpensive craft—one that's fun for all age groups, then rock craft may be just right for you. People have always found uses—both practical and decorative—for rocks and pebbles. Rocks in unusual natural shapes often had a religious significance. And, since that day long ago when one of our prehistoric ancestors had the bright idea of decorating his or her home, it was doubtless a rock, attractive because of color or shape, that became the first dust-gathering knickknack in some primeval cave.

When man or woman first turned his or her hand to an art form more permanent than drawing in sand with a stick, rocks, because they were readily available, were both implement and material. They have remained a material for sculptors ever since because of their beauty and permanence.

Most early creative attempts, scratched with a hard stone into the soft chalk or sandstone walls of a cliff face or cave, have probably long since eroded into oblivion. But some, including those decorated with earth colors, remain to be seen in various parts of the world.

Early sculptors, with the primitive tools available to them, used rocks pretty much as they found them. They made minimal changes, if any, to produce symbolic figures and forms. With the development of metal tools and more skilled craftsmen, this art form developed by slow stages to the ideal beauty of Classical and Renaissance sculpture and later to the photographic realism evidence in nineteenth- and early twentieth-century bronzes.

Many contemporary sculptors, concluding that realism has reached a perfection that cannot be improved upon, have returned to symbolism. We seem to have come full circle to the simplified forms which are pure design and the abstracts in which it is apparent that the artist is having fun with his craft.

The rock craft projects described in this book are not lofty works of art, but they are fun. They utilize pebbles, stones, and rocks, just as they are found, to create various decorative formats that are as enjoyable for the rock crafter to do as they are for others to look at. They use rocks in combination with other odds and ends to create all sorts of strange forms. And they take advantage of such modern aids as acrylic paints, white glue, epoxy glue, and felt-tipped pens to enhance shapes and decorate found forms.

Pebble Pets and People is a book about a craft that's fun for just about any age group. It is educational too, in that it helps children develop some simple craft skills. But, perhaps better yet, it allows their imaginations free reign to see forms and faces in pebbles and stones they might pick up anywhere.

Even the youngest artists can't come to too much harm with nontoxic acrylic paints and felt-tipped pens. But when they explore the joys of making rock assemblies using epoxy glue and other materials, it is advisable to give a few words of caution or, better yet, to be on hand to supervise from a noninterfering distance.

For the rock crafter who can let imagination run free, there is no end to the wonders waiting in the rocks of the seashore, the garden, or the street. He just needs an eye constantly on the lookout for the raw materials. And those materials can range from a pebble the size of a pinhead to a rock the size of a gallon jug. The secret is in your own imagination and in what you can create from your rocks with a few deft touches.

Rocks can be turned into pretty pets or peculiar people. It all depends on you. Rocks can be pictures, centerpieces, groupings, message carriers, or just nice things to fondle. Whatever you begin with, a few hours of fun will produce an array of designs, fantasy figures, or odd-looking animals that will delight you. And when you or your children have had the fun of making wild designs, people, animals, or the monsters that children seem to love creating, you'll find they are welcome gifts for friends. What's more, if you happen to be business minded and can bear to part with your creations, you'll find a ready market for them at school or church bazaars, flea markets, and perhaps even gift shops.

I hope this book will give you a few ideas on directions in which you might want to experiment. It surely will not exhaust all the possibilities, because people see rocks so differently and every rock is different—just waiting for someone to discover its real potential.

GETTING STARTED

Did you think that pebbles were just small rocks that are hard on bare feet? So did I before they started to turn into zany characters to delight my family and friends. Now, whenever I wander on the beach or in a park, I find myself ambling head down, risking collisions, always on the lookout for interesting specimens. I seldom return home from a stroll without pockets bulging with goodies to add to my growing store of raw materials for rock crafting.

This is a simple craft if you want it to be, but it can also be as complex as you care to make it. And certainly you couldn't find a craft that costs much less to pursue. Most of the basic bits and pieces you'll need are just lying around waiting to be picked up.

Anyone who has ever sat on a beach or a pebbled patio

11

must have casually picked up odd-shaped stones and pebbles worn into a myriad of interesting shapes. There is something down-to-earth and basically satisfying in holding a nice smooth stone in your hand, turning it this way and that. The Japanese and Chinese know the value of good-looking stones. They use them in attractive gardens where such stones set off plants beautifully.

Sitting and looking at your pebbles is part of the craft too, whether you meditate or not, for you will find, once you have collected an assortment of interestingly shaped pebbles, that the more you look at them, the more they almost tell you what they would like to be.

There is probably greater variety in rocks and pebbles than in just about any other substance on earth—and perhaps this is why they are so interesting. No two are ever quite alike, either in shape, color, texture, or grain. Many are so beautiful just as nature made them that it seems almost a crime to change them in any way. For such naturally beautiful specimens, you just have to find the right setting.

The basis of their beauty may be color, surface texture, or shape. Stones can be beautiful even if they are not of the precious or semiprecious variety. I have a magnificent piece of green stone from Colorado weighing about three hundred pounds sitting in a small entrance garden. It's just the way my wife and I found it—rough, diamond shaped, and beautiful—and I almost broke my back getting it home. But it's a source of great pleasure to us and to many visiting friends. My wife also has small, attractive pebbles that she uses in flower arrangements. The point I'm making is that even if you don't decorate them or turn them into people or pets, pebbles and stones can be worthwhile just to look at. They have a tranquilizing permanence.

This book is not really about such "pet" rocks as these, used as nature left them. Rather it explores ways to embellish ordinary stones by combining a number of them to create fantasy creatures or by decorating a single stone to make it an attractive solo piece.

The pebbles or rocks you collect for this craft can be any color or shape. The only rule is that if you want to paint or decorate them, their surfaces should be smooth, or relatively so. Otherwise you'll find them difficult to work with.

Go to your source of stones, whether that be the beach, your patio, garden, local park, or your general neighborhood looking for pebbles and rocks of various sizes. Or, if you're really stuck, you can usually buy nice smooth pebbles in florists' shops and garden centers. That really shouldn't be necessary, however, when you think of all the stones just lying about the earth, so let's discount it except as a last resort.

WHAT TO LOOK FOR

Rocks, Pebbles, and Stones

Pick up any pebbles small enough to fit in your pocket or whatever receptacle you have along for the purpose. A good idea is to carry a small plastic bag about with you to put pebbles in—you never know when or where you're going to find them. Sometimes they have dirt, oil, or tar on them that you don't notice, which tends to make a nasty mess in the pocket. When you get your pebbles home, wash and dry them, because dirt or dust will stop paint or glue from adhering properly. At the same time, a nice bath spruces them up—they're just like people—and you may find unexpected beauties of color and texture.

Among the stones you collect, round ones (rather rare) will make good heads for people—but you can use oval or slightly tapering ones just as well. And if you have to use some other odd shape for a head, you're just going to end up with a more grotesque figure, which works out fine, too. Oval or pear-shaped stones make good bodies.

Flat ones make good feet if they are small and elongated. If they are bigger, they are useful for message stones, pictures, or découpage. Skinny sausage shapes make eels or worms. Humpbacked stones with one flat side to sit on are ideal for cats, turtles, owls, or almost any reclining animal form.

Just bear in mind that when you're out collecting rocks and pebbles, it's not important to look for specific shapes, but rather to pick up anything you find—especially if it's smooth. From the collection you assemble, you'll discover that uses will suggest themselves. And the more you become involved with this intriguing craft, the more easily ideas will come to you.

If the natural color or grain of a stone appeals to you, it may look great just cleaned up and varnished. Or you might use a number of plain, unpainted stones to make a pebble picture. The same grouping could of course be painted to add additional character to the individual figures. Almost any pebble you pick up will spring to life with some personality of its own if you stare at it long enough from different directions, or just live with it for a while. Some days seem to be more creative, for me at least, when it comes to seeing a stone for what it could best become.

Other Materials

The purist will stay with pebbles and rocks alone. But if you care to add a few other bits and pieces, such as beads, buttons, bits of glass, wire, wood, dried seeds, felt, fur, découpage, and so on, the possibilities are almost endless.

If you start by decorating an individual stone, you'll need only paints and a brush, or felt-tipped pens, and artist's fixative or varnish to protect the finished designs. A single color felt-tipped pen can do a wonderful job. In that case, it really all depends upon the design you give it.

If you start by assembling people or animals, you'll need epoxy glue. In some instances, white glue will do to hold pebbles together. In chapter 5, "Especially for Children," you'll find assorted things to do using white glue which is easier and safer for children than epoxy, although it takes longer to dry.

To show how inexpensive and accessible rock craft is, here is a list of the things you'll need to make a simple, basic pebble person. The same list goes for more complicated projects, too. If you're going to use only single rocks rather than multi-pebble assemblies, you'll just need something to decorate them with, and varnish for a protective finish coat. But I suspect you'll want to go further than that. So here's the basic list, to which you'll add your own odds and ends and household scraps as you develop the craft in your own unique way.

Counterclockwise from right: Roll of household foil; roll of ½-inch masking tape; lid to mix glue on; stick to mix glue with; tubes of epoxy glue.

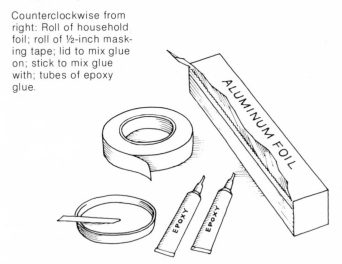

Basic Supplies

- Pebbles

- Quick-setting epoxy glue, *not* regular epoxy (What you want is the sort that's called five-minute epoxy.)

- White glue for most of the children's projects

- An old tin lid with a clean metal surface on which to mix epoxy glue

- A couple of wooden kitchen matches, or slivers of wood about that size, with which to mix the epoxy glue and apply it to the pebbles

- Some extra stones, wood blocks, jars, bottles, or things like that to support your figures while the glue sets

- Some masking tape for the same purpose—to hold pebbles in position while the glue sets. (Tape ½" wide is best. You'll find the wider tape gets in the way.)

- A jar of gesso, which you can get in an art or craft supply store. (This will smooth out minor imperfections in a pebble or rock, give you a better surface on which to paint or draw and, because it's white, will make all your colors brighter when you paint them over it.)

Clockwise from left:
Tubes of acrylic paint;
jar of gloss polymer
medium; felt-tip pens;
pencil; brush.

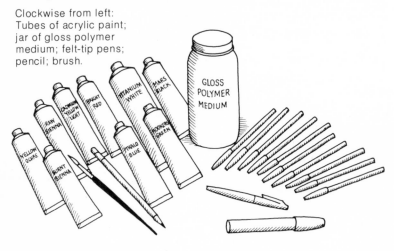

- Some acrylic water-base paints in the colors you want to use. (Make sure your selection includes the primaries—red, blue and yellow—plus black and white and yellow ochre. You will find the yellow ochre necessary for skin tones.)

- An artist's watercolor brush, preferably size 2. (Get a good one, because you need a brush that will hold a fine point for drawing lines.)

- A selection of felt-tipped pens, including some with fine tips for detail. (Get the waterproof sort if you can, so the colors won't run when you use polymer medium or varnish over them. If you use water-soluble colors, spray the design with artist's fixative before or instead of varnishing.)

- A cookie sheet, piece of scrap glass, or metal can lid to mix your acrylic paints on

- Acrylic polymer gloss medium. (This will give you a shiny finish when you're all through painting. You can either mix it with your colors as you use them or paint it over the whole finished piece like varnish. While not essential, this finish protects the paint from dirt and possible smudging and gives a nice gloss. It also makes the piece waterproof enough to wipe off dirt and dust that might accumulate with time. If you prefer a matte look to a glossy finish, you can use either matte medium or matte acrylic varnish.)

- A spray can of artist's fixative, in case you find yourself working with water-soluble colors.

This book is not laid out as a course for you to work your way through. Rather, each project is self-sufficient, although some may refer you back to a method or skill explained in some previous project, rather than waste space by explaining the concept over again.

We suggest that before you open paint pots or mix glue to start any project that appeals to you, you read through the explanatory steps about that project completely, end to end, and more than once if necessary to make sure you understand what is to be done. Most of the steps are simple, but a few are tricky to explain in words, even though they are easy once understood and mastered. However, please don't worry about it, because this is one of the few crafts I know—and I've dabbled in most—where even your mistakes can be fun.

The only satisfactory way to join pebbles together is with epoxy glue. White glue, which is safer for youngsters, is fine for sticking other porous materials to the stones, but it does not make a permanent, hard, rock-to-rock bond. That is why the projects for children in this book, do not involve joining stones together. This is not to say that children cannot have the fun of multi-pebble creations, but if epoxy is involved, an adult should be on hand to mix and apply it, or at least to supervise if you feel they are safe to use it alone. It is difficult to put a safe age on any dangerous substance or article such as craft knives and razor blades. It is a responsible age rather than a chronological one that counts here. The adult who turns this book over to any child must be the judge of what his or her particular young craftsman is capable of.

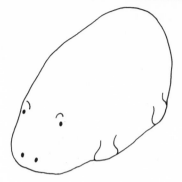

19

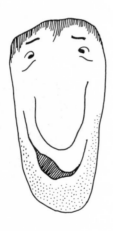

FOUND ROCK CHARACTERS

Perhaps the easiest way of getting hooked on rock craft is to start with a single pebble rather than an assembly. Among the rocks you gather there will be some that suggest something to you all on their own. Or they may be beautiful, flat, smooth rocks that make ideal painting or decorating surfaces but lack the lumps and bumps that make for interesting three-dimensional characters. And, as with all rocks, it is sometimes necessary to live with them for a while until some inspired idea for their use comes to you.

Individual rocks can be turned into various animal forms, real or imaginary. Or you can paint designs on them (from nature or otherwise) if they don't suggest anything in particular to you. In most cases, unless your rock is a very pale color, it is best to paint it white first, either with acrylic paint or gesso. Because it is thick, and tends to fill in and smooth out any slight imperfections, gesso is especially useful if the rock has a slightly rough surface.

Sometimes it is possible to use the basic color of your rock as the background color for your creation. It all depends on the effect you want to create. One nice thing about using acrylic colors for rock painting is that they dry fast so that you don't have a lot of waiting time. Also, if you goof, it's easy to paint out the whole thing with white paint or gesso and start over again.

ABOUT PAINTING

At this stage, perhaps a word about painting on rocks is in order. You'll find that either acrylic paints or felt-tipped pens will do the job, especially if you start with a white gesso base. Most likely, you'll end up using a combination of the two. I usually use acrylics for the big areas of color, or bright spots, and felt-tipped pens for fine details and lines on top of the acrylics. Pens are easier to use than brushes for fine line work, unless you are an accomplished brush user. Just be sure to test them before you start using them on a stone. Some have a tendency to run, or they may be dry and make an uneven line to begin with. Another point about pens is that to get the color shown on their caps, you must work on a white surface. Because they are usually transparent colors, they will be virtually invisible on a dark surface. If you use them on top of any other color, you will get a shade that's a combination of the pen and base colors.

If you're using acrylic paints, check the tops of the tubes or jars before you begin to make sure you can get them off easily. It's very frustrating not to be able to get into a color when you need it. If you don't have a pair of pliers or bottle opening gadget handy, an easy alternative is to use any door. In case you don't know that trick, here's how it works. Go to any door that opens away from you. Open it and hold the handle in one hand and the tube of paint in the other, with your fingers on the solid part at the top of the tube near the cap.

Now put the cap into the hinge side of the door opening and gently close the door toward you, so that the edges of the cap are touching the edge of the door and the side trim of the door frame. Pull on the door gently, just enough to hold the tube cap tight, and at the same time give the tube a counterclockwise twist. It will usually loosen the cap like a charm. Just a word of caution, however. If you pull too hard on the door, you'll dent the door and the trim. If you don't pull hard enough, the cap will turn with the tube and act like a file on your door and molding.

Once you have the top off, it's a good idea to scrub out the cap with water and a nail brush before putting it on again. And always wipe off any excess paint from the top of your tube before putting the cap back.

If you don't already have acrylic paints on hand, go to the store and buy the cheapest set you can find from the children's department. You can usually get a small set of acrylic tube paints for a few dollars. At the same time, get a set of felt-tipped pens in assorted colors—with fine tips, so you can draw thin lines. They won't cost more than a couple of dollars, either, for the water-soluble kind. Pens with waterproof ink will be more expensive. Make sure the acrylic set you buy includes black, white, red, yellow, blue, and yellow ochre. If it happens to have other colors, so much the better, but you can always mix your own if you have the primaries. The white and yellow ochre are essential for light skin tones and the black for outlines and assorted other features. Adding red, yellow, and blue will make darker skin tones depending on the quantity of each color added.

Brushes

The brushes that come in children's paint sets are usually no good at all (which is tough on kids who want to paint, when you think of it) because you can't draw a fine line with them.

The hairs on cheap brushes seldom come to a good point, and if they do, they tend to separate too easily, making it harder to paint both fine lines and flat areas of color. They usually shed hairs easily, too, and hairs are hard to get off a small painted pebble. So splurge on at least one good quality artist's watercolor brush. A size 2 may cost you a dollar or so, but it's well worth it in terms of the frustration it will avoid. And with acrylic paints, where you can easily wash the brush in water between colors, one brush is enough to work with.

ROCK CREATIONS

Getting back to our individual rock creations, here are a few suggestions for what you might do with them. Perhaps the very easiest way to start is with a one-color design drawn on a nice, smooth, light-colored rock. Such a piece is shown here. The stone we started with was a smooth but irregularly shaped pebble that was almost dead white in color. I'm not sure what sort of stone it is, geologically speaking, but I suspect marble or feldspar. It was found on the beach. When it was wet, it had an attractive translucent look that made me

The simplest form of rock craft is to decorate a single stone with black felt-tip pen as shown here, then varnish it with gloss polymer medium.

One-Color Design

want to preserve its natural color. For that reason, the simple floral designs on it are drawn with a waterproof black felt-tipped pen. They are drawn, like a photographic negative, in reverse, with the natural color of the stone showing through as lines to indicate veins. I did it that way to make the design bolder than it would have been in outline. When the design was finished, I gave the stone a coat of acrylic polymer gloss medium which, because it dries shiny, brought out the original translucent look the stone had when wet.

If you want to try decorating a rock this way, but feel unsure of your design or your ability to put it on directly, try out a few pen strokes and designs on paper first. Then copy it onto your rock. Don't be nervous about it. Firm confident strokes look better than timid ones even if they're not quite where you originally intended them to be. And if you don't like your finished piece, you can always give it a couple of coats of white acrylic paint and start over again. That's one of the joys of rock painting.

Permanent Greeting Card

Permanent Greeting Cards
The finished Valentine rock. Actual size is about 3½" top to bottom.

If it happens to be near Christmas, Easter, Valentine's Day, or someone's birthday when you get the urge to paint a rock, here's something that's fun to do and as personalized as you want to make it. We show here a Valentine's Day rock, but the basic technique is the same, whatever the occasion.

25

1. Find a flat rock big enough for your message and any design embellishments you have in mind. It doesn't matter if the edges of your stone are rough or smooth, as long as one surface at least is smooth enough to paint and write on. Lay your rock on

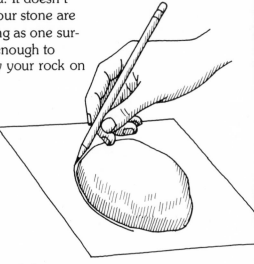

a piece of white paper and draw a line around the edge of it, so you have its shape outlined on the paper.
2. Now paint the side of the rock that will carry your message with white acrylic paint or gesso.
3. Put it aside to dry while you work out the message and design placement inside the outline pattern you've drawn on paper. This will probably take you long enough for the white

base coat to dry. If you start with a
dark-colored stone, you may find that
a second coat of white is necessary to
make the color solid and give you an
even base to work on. Paint the
edges of your rock as well—and the
back, too, if you like—though this
isn't entirely necessary. If you want
some color other than white for a
base color, paint this on top of your
gesso coat and leave it to dry also.
Remember that it should be a pale
color if your design and writing are to
show up well.

3. When you have the message and design worked out to your satisfaction,
copy them onto the stone, using either felt-tipped pens or acrylic paints
and your fine-tipped brush. Put the
message on first, followed by the design, since you can always adjust the
size of the design to fit the space left
after the message is on.

When painting the design—and
this applies to any painting as a general rule—you'll find it best to start
with the areas of light color first and
work through progressively darker
colors, ending up with black outlines, if
you are going to use them. Black outlines between colors are a great help
to amateur artists like me, who tend
to end up with ragged-edged colors.
With a felt-tipped pen, you can draw
black lines easily and evenly to cover
up a multitude of minor errors in the
colors underneath.

4. After your design is dry, either spray
it with a coat of artist's fixative or give
it a coat of acrylic varnish or polymer
medium—matte or glossy to your
taste. Remember that if you have
used water-soluble inks in making
your design, you'll have to spray

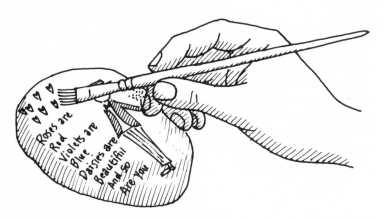

them with a fixative before you varnish. Varnish applied directly will
make the colors run.

5. The back of the stone can either be
painted the same color as the front,
have additional designs or messages
(a post-script might be appropriate),
or be left natural. It's probably best to
spray or varnish the same as the front
so the color looks consistent. And for
safety, if you've left the back blank,
glue a piece of felt on it to protect any
surface it might be placed on.

Rock with decoupaged
illustration and felt pen
message.

28

Découpaged Rocks

As an alternative to painting on a design, or if you feel too unsure of yourself to try freehand painting, you can découpage a design or picture onto your flat stone. Découpage is the art of decorating a surface with paper cutouts. When this technique is used on a rock, a piece of furniture, or some other article, it appears that the design has been painted on by hand.

1. Start as before with a white-painted or gessoed stone. The stone needs to be flat enough so that your cutout paper design will lie flat on it without wrinkling.
2. Now cut out your design, picture, or message from an old calendar, greeting card, or whatever. The thinner the paper, the more it will look as if it were painted on the stone instead of glued on. Professionals at découpage cut their designs right to the edge of the print so no background paper shows, but you can always paint the edges of your découpaged design paper with acrylics after the design is set, to match the background color of your rock.
3. Attach your picture, design, or message to the stone with white glue.

When it's dry, and you have applied any finishing touches or other design elements you want to add, coat it with polymer gloss medium or acrylic varnish.

The two découpaged rocks shown in Color Plate 9 are painted white with gesso and the design glued on. The one shown on page 28 in black and white is painted with a blue and green background to simulate ground and sky. The two colors are merged together where they meet by keeping the colors wet and thin so that they run together. The message on this latter was added with a felt tipped pen after the design was in place. Waterproof ink was used, so it wasn't necessary to spray with artist's fixative before giving the whole rock its final shiny coat with polymer gloss medium.

If you don't want the edges of your picture or message to show up as a ridge when they're glued on—which may happen if the paper from which you cut your design is thick—you can rub them down on the back with very fine sandpaper, to get a wafer-thin edge before you stick them on. Be careful not to sand right through your paper and remove part of the design. The only safe way to do it is to put your découpage design on an absolutely flat surface—a piece of glass is best—and, with your very fine sandpaper wrapped around the tip of your finger, gently rub the edges of the

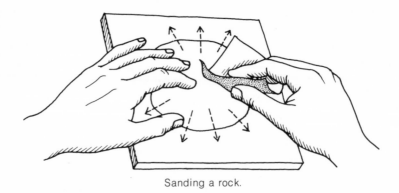

Sanding a rock.

30

design, working out toward the edge of the paper with each stroke. It's best to practice this first on a piece of scrap paper that's left over when you cut out your design.

Don't use magazine pages to cut your pictures from if you plan to varnish your finished piece with découpage varnish or any spirit-base varnish. They almost always have something printed on the other side, and whatever is printed on the back will probably show through the front. If, however, you are content to give your découpage its shiny coat by using acrylic polymer gloss medium, chances are it will be safe. To be certain, it's always best to do a small test first, using a scrap piece of the same paper you intend to use for your design cutout. Glue it to anything with white glue and give it a coat of acrylic polymer gloss medium. If nothing shows through when it dries—and drying takes only a few minutes—it's safe to go ahead with your project.

Designs cut from wallpaper can be used for découpage. So can photos, if you're careful and do the test mentioned above first. Most craft stores carry designs printed expressly for découpage and even découpage transfers. Transfers, of course, are no thicker than the ink they are printed with and are thus perfect, since there is no edge line. However, to use transfers for rock découpage, you need a perfectly smooth stone, or you will not get a complete transfer when you apply it and will end up with missing pieces where there are dents or holes in your stone.

You can purchase special découpage varnish at craft supply stores, but it has two drawbacks. First, there is the danger that anything printed on the back of your design will show through. The second problem is that découpage varnish is much slower to dry than acrylic medium. The reason for using it in regular découpage is to build up a thick layer of varnish by adding coat upon coat—sometimes as many as twenty. This gives a thick enough varnish coat that you can smooth out any paper ridges that show after the first few coats with sandpaper or steel wool. It also gives a beautiful depth to the final shine, but it's a long, slow process.

ABSTRACT DESIGNS

Abstract designs and simple native motifs copied from many cultures can make attractive single rock decorations. Abstracts can be as wild as your imagination allows. Start with a white base color and draw on swirls and curls conforming more or less to the shape of your stone. Or fill in patches of different colors, again following the general shape and contour of your stone. If you have any books on native American art (and if you don't, your local library surely will), you'll find a wealth of source material of simple designs that can be adapted for rock painting. An example of such a rock is the Mexcian design that follows.

A Mexican Design
(See also Color Plate 2)

This design is adapted from a standard Mexican design motif commonly called "the shouting pheasant." It illustrates how, with a little artistic license, almost any design can be made to fit a rock of almost any shape with the addition of a few extra lines and curls. The rock was a little rough, so I first applied three coats

Abstract design made to fit shape of stone and drawn entirely with colored felt-tip pens.

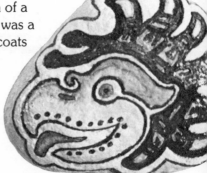

Mexican Design

32

of gesso to smooth out the holes and crevices before the design went on. I then painted it using only felt-tipped pens with water-soluble colors. Because of this, the design was sprayed with artist's fixative to stop the colors from running. A final coat of acrylic polymer gloss medium was added to make the finished piece shine.

A Fishy Friend

(See also Color Plate 2)

Since fish come in just about every size and shape in their natural state, they are also natural subjects for flights of fantasy in individual rock or pebble decoration. If you have ever looked at pictures of those creatures who seem to prefer life several miles deep down in the ocean, you'll know what I mean by virtually un-limited shapes. Many of them look so fantastic, you'd think they just had to have been dreamed up by some crazy rock crafter. But even the more normal fish shapes, with their bulging eyes, are naturals for re-creation in rocks and pebbles. And their scales make an attrac-tive, easily simulated decorative pattern.

To make one, proceed as follows:

1. Paint your pebble all over with white or some other light color base paint.
2. Work out your design for your fish's face, fins, and scales on paper.
3. With fine brush and acrylic paint, or fine-point felt-tipped pens, put in mouth, eyes, eyebrows, and fins.
4. Add scales using either your pens or the acrylic paint.

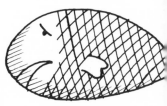

As with all rock or pebble painting, it's simpler and usually more effective not to strive for too much realism in your designs. Use what is in effect a cartoon style—or at least simplify your subject. Consider designs created for needlepoint as an inspirational source of style. They are done in what might be termed "simplified realism."

Examples of how easily a few lines can change the expression on a fish's face. Also shown: Two methods of drawing scales with fine lines.

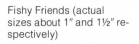
Fishy Friends (actual sizes about 1" and 1½" respectively)

A Lovable Ladybug

(See also Color Plate 2)

Ladybug (actual size about 2½" long). Note the use of black paint at the base of the piece to give the look of an even bottom. The base of this rock (a round one split in half) was very rough and irregular.

If you come across a smallish, hump-backed stone—sort of hemispherical—it will make an ideal ladybug. Sometimes you'll find a half pebble that got split somehow so that it is round on the top and flat on the bottom. Don't discard it. Here is your ladybug. (Or if it's too big for the ladybug you have in mind, it might be a crouching pussycat. Or if it's slightly pointy at one end, you've got yourself the makings of an interesting hedgehog.)

1. First, if it is a darkish stone to begin with, paint it white all over. Since ladybugs are brightly colored creatures, you need to have your colors show up well.

35

2. The main feature of a ladybug, to make it recognizable as such even in its rock variety, are its rounded shape and the division of the wings. Paint these features so that they really show up. Accentuate the eyes. Eyes are a very important feature in any rock craft creature. They turn them into characters rather than just animals, a fact that the early cartoon movie creators recognized.

An Owl to Ogle You

(See also Color Plate 3)

Another simple-to-make but very effective rock creature is an owl.

1. Because of an owl's shape, the ideal stone is an oval one that's flat enough on one end to stand up. If you find one that's the right shape, but won't quite stand alone, you can help out by sanding, filing, or grinding down the end the owl is to sit on. This isn't easy with a hard rock, unless you happen to have a power operated grindstone. So if you have to take this step, it's best to start with a rock that's soft, like sandstone. Then rub it back and forth on a file or on very coarse sandpaper on a flat surface until it will stand unsupported. Alter-

natively, and more easily, you can use a blob of epoxy glue. Just prop your pebble on one end on a blob of epoxy mixed on a piece of foil paper and let it dry there. When you peel off the foil, you'll have a small neat "foot" for your owl to stand on.

2. The eyes are the most important part of any owl—they glow at you out of the dark. And between those staring eyes, you have to give the suggestion of a short, sharp beak. The colors can be anything your imagination conjures up, but a dark body will make those owlish eyes pop out at you more effectively. Owl's eyes, like cat's eyes, can either have slits or circles for pupils.

Single pebble owl (actual size about 1″ side to side). Only the eyes are really important.

The owl shown in the black and white picture on the right is made from half of a flat, oval pebble. It was broken flat enough to stand alone when I found it. I first painted two circles for the eyes with white acrylic, then put pale yellow over the white to make the yellow glow. A small beak between the eyes was similarly painted, first with white and then orange. The rest of the pebble was given a coat of burnt sienna brown as a base. Then, with a waterproof black felt-tipped pen, I drew circles around the eyes, vertical slits to make pupils, the outline of his beak, and the feathers with a series of U-shaped lines.

The Zanies or Crazies

(See also Color Plate 6)

These are wild or weird creatures that don't fit into any other category. They usually have some slight human or animal look which takes them out of the abstract design grouping.

How do you make one? Well, a wild imagination helps, but to be more precise, they are created by unusual or unexpected combinations of natural features: a foot with a face attached, a huge eye with nothing else, a tree with heads or eyes instead of fruit, flowers with faces, and so on. Almost any unusual combination of elements will create a zany character.

Whatever you may call the creatures in these pictures, they are flights of fancy or imagination, painted with acrylics on individual rocks, created mainly for the enjoyment of the person painting them. But they can also become conversation pieces if you leave them lying around your home when friends are coming.

The black paint which outlines the toes on this piece also becomes the hair around the head.

Zanies

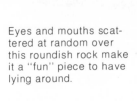

Eyes and mouths scattered at random over this roundish rock make it a "fun" piece to have lying around.

38

Chirpy Chicks
(See also Color Plate 5)

Come Easter time, you might want to create a chirpy chick to add to an Easter basket or give as a gift on its own. It's probably best to put one in a basket of straw or excelsior among a bunch of Easter eggs for some young friend. My daughter made these originally from single pebbles, but at the last minute, after they were all painted and varnished, she decided that they should have feet as well, which she added by tucking a couple of tiny pebbles under their tummies and fixing them there with white glue. The predominant colors are yellow and orange dabbed on in a random fashion, with yellow beaks, black eyes, and a few black lines for accents.

A pair of chicks, or birds, showing how two sizes of the same design can look attractive together. The bigger bird is about 3″ high. They are white, with yellow and orange blobs, and black lines for detail.

39

Snails and Worms

(See also Color Plate 2)

Snails and worms are natural single-pebble shapes. While you might think of snails and worms as rather objectionable slimy creatures, they do make rather attractive subjects for pebble creatures. Almost any long cylindrical sort of pebble will make a great worm—or caterpillar, if you find that a more attractive thought. And any humpbacked stone will make a snail, where the hump can become the house every snail carries around on his back.

HOW TO MAKE A WORM

1. First paint your stone white. While it dries, work out your design on paper.
2. Now paint on your palest colors first and work your way progressively through to darker shades, letting each color dry before you paint the next.
3. If you want the colors to bleed into each other in bands, paint the second area of color while the first paint is still wet, working back toward the first and painting over the edge of the first color, letting the colors merge where they meet. Don't work the opposite way or you'll get mixed colors in your paint brush and no clear color bands at all.

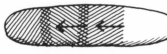

First band of color.

Rock showing progression of bands of color.

4. Using a black felt-tipped pen or black
   paint, draw on facial features and, if
   you wish, draw black lines around
   areas of color to make them stand
   out distinctly rather than having
   blended bands of color.

HOW TO MAKE A SNAIL

You'll need a humpbacked stone. Then,
decorate it as if you were making a
worm, but add the bump shape for his
back.

1. If the stone is a dark color, paint it all
   over with white first. Draw your design on paper within an outline of the
   shape of your stone. The shell outline
   should be curved at the bottom.
2. Paint the shell before you paint the
   body, using a light color.
3. Paint the design on the snail's body.
4. Using a black felt-tipped pen or black
   acrylic paint, outline the areas of
   color and all facial features.

Side and top views:
Suggested design for
snail.

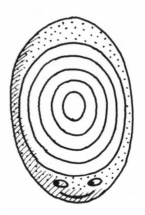

The Love-Sick Lady Whale

(See also Color Plate 12)

This heart-spouting, lovelorn lady was painted on the flatter side of a piece of split shale rock. Actually, it was a very rough-surfaced piece. Its shape suggested a whale when I found it, so it seemed worth the attempt. She was made using felt-tipped pens with water-soluble colors for all decoration.

Lady Whale

A very rough piece of shale rock, painted entirely with felt tip pens, showing how a design can be made to fit in your rock, whatever its shape.

1. Because it was a very rough piece of shale, I gave it three coats of gesso to fill in the holes and to make the surface smooth enough to paint on. If you start with a smooth stone, you won't have to do this.

42

2. The next step, as in most single rock designs, is to draw the outline of your rock on paper and work out a design within that space. Remember, you can curl your whale's tail any way necessary to fit your rock.

3. The first thing to draw on your rock is the outline of the whale. Then add the outline of the side fins, eyelid, and eyelashes.

4. Now, with a red pen, add the lips and the small circles and dots on the lower part of the body to suggest scales.

5. Using a blue-green pen, draw the slightly wavy lines that simulate the sea. Make them almost solid at the bottom, thinning out toward the top. With the same pen, draw broken curving lines out from the whale's spout or blow hole, leaving spaces where you'll put the hearts. You can also paint in a blue-green eye.

6. Draw tiny hearts in the gaps in the lines, keeping the point of each heart pointing back toward the whale and in line with the blue-green lines.

7. With an assortment of colors, draw the irregular color patches on the head, back and tail, arranging them so that the colors are well mixed, with no two patches of similar color adjoining. Don't let the colored patches touch anywhere; leave some background color showing.

8. The last coloring is done with a dark blue pen. Just draw a series of dots on the side and tail fin, the first ones

widely spaced, the others gradually
getting closer to each other, finally
touching, and therefore solid color, at
the fin tips.

9. You can now apply artist's fixative. If,
however, you are not quite satisfied
with your whale, you can paint it over
with gesso and start again.

And with that, I leave the field of single rock decorating. It is the simplest form of the craft, yet offers plenty of scope for your imagination. And there are hundreds of designs in books, magazines, and newspapers that you can turn to for ideas.

ASSEMBLED ROCK CHARACTERS

Joining pebbles and rocks together with epoxy glue before painting them provides almost limitless potential for creating figures, animals, and wild shapes. Using stones of almost any shape and size, you'll find that the scope is as wide as your imagination and supply of stones. Perhaps the best place to start is with a human figure. Here is how to go about assembling your basic pebble person.

First, though, a word about epoxy glue. Five-minute epoxy glue means just that, so don't worry about a lot of time wasted waiting for glue to dry. If you're working on several figures at once, you can switch back and forth among them and not waste a moment. Your biggest problem will probably be using up the glue before it hardens.

The sort of epoxy I use comes in two tubes, one containing glue, the other a hardener. You put equal quantities of glue and hardener side by side, or hardener on top of glue, then stir them together with a small piece of stick. I usually do this on the bottom of an empty fruit juice can or some other can rescued from the garbage. It makes a clean steady surface and the can is easily disposed of. Although you can mix succeeding batches of glue on top of each other, it's better to find a clean spot on the can each time, so you can see where the fresh glue is. Because of the speed at which epoxy glue dries, that's a consideration. After you've mixed it, you have two or three minutes to work before it starts to set and becomes useless.

BASIC PEBBLE PERSON

The simplest figure is made of just four or five pebbles: a large one to make a body, a middle-sized one for a head, and two small flattish ones for feet. The fifth stone should be really tiny, to make a nose, if you want your person to have one.

Five pebbles for basic pebble person.

46

ASSEMBLED ROCK CHARACTERS

Noses on rock people look best on old men, crones, and witches. Let's assume your pebble person will have a nose. Don't worry if you can't find stones that are absolutely smooth or perfectly symmetrical. Grotesque shapes tend to produce more interesting people.

1. Look for a body stone roughly egg shaped and about three inches long, a head stone roughly round or oval and about an inch in diameter, two foot stones about an inch long and a quarter to half an inch wide, and a tiny round or pyramid-shaped one for a nose. If you can't find pebbles of these actual sizes, look for a group in about the same proportions. Don't worry about getting them exactly right. If the head is too big or too small it just adds to the unique look of the finished figure.
2. Tear off a piece of household foil and lay the two stones for the feet down on it, touching each other at some point. If any epoxy glue runs down the sides of your foot stones, it will just set flat at the bottom. (You can peel off the foil when the glue is dry.) It helps to make a flat base, so that your figure can stand upright. The foil also prevents bleached-out marks or blobs of glue on your working surface—or a pebble person permanently attached to the middle of your dining room table.

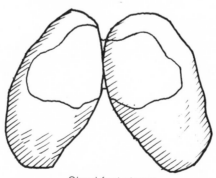

Glued foot stones.

3. Once you have put the two foot stones down on the foil, just touching each other, put the body stone on them so that it touches both foot stones. Now find some suitable props to hold the body in the position you want on the foot stones. Small cans or jars, other stones, or blocks of wood serve just fine for this. They just have to let you prop the body more or less upright in the position you selected. Again, don't worry too much about it as long as the body is more or less upright.

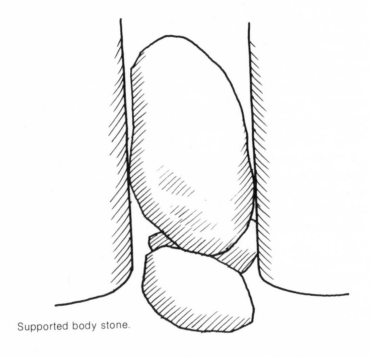

Supported body stone.

4. Now you're ready to glue, following the directions on your epoxy. If it's two-tube epoxy (glue and hardener), mix about enough to cover a dime. Be stingy with your glue squeezing, since it's the most expensive part of the craft and you'll probably throw away more than you use anyway. Put a blob of glue on each foot where the body will rest, and drop anything left over between the two feet

stones to hold them together. Plant the body back into position, propped up with the supports you selected. Make sure that the feet stick out a bit behind the body, because that will help ensure that your figure stands alone when the supports are removed. Leave it for five minutes, which is about all the time necessary for the new, fast-drying epoxy glue to set. It won't be dried completely hard, but it will be set enough to take the supports away. Then it will harden while you continue with the next stage.

5. Now you are ready to attach the head. This can either sit straight on top of the body or slope down at an angle, as shown on the cave man, circus rider, and accountant. Again, either find some suitable objects to hold it in that position, or use masking tape to hold it. Personally, I find masking tape easier and quicker for this stage. Tear off a couple of strips long enough to go right across the head in the form of a cross and attach to the body at front, back, and sides. Then put a blob of epoxy on the body where the head is to attach and spread it around so it covers an area about the size of a nickel. Do the same thing to the head stone at the point you plan to attach it to the body. Then attach the head to the body with the masking tape and let the glue harden.

Taped head stone.

49

The reason for spreading the glue a bit is that, while epoxy glue only needs a very thin layer to hold, the stone may not be as strong. It's quite possible for the two stones to break apart, taking off a small layer of stone as they do so. Spreading the glue around a bit makes a wider, stronger holding joint.

Don't worry about the glue showing. If you're going to paint the figure with acrylics or a coat of gesso before using felt-tipped pens, none of this excess glue will show at all. If it turns out that you've been extra generous with the glue and some runs down the body and dries there, that's no great calamity either. You can always paint a glue blob to look like a choker or the end of a scarf or something. But if excess glue bothers you, just use the minimum amount of glue at first to set the head, and add more when the first lot is dry.

6. The next step's the nose. Take your nose stone and place it with a spot of epoxy in the middle of the front of your head stone. Remember that the eyes you'll paint in later will be level with the top of the nose. You'll need space above the eyes and nose for a forehead, so don't place the nose too near the top. Hold the nose in position with masking tape (lightly) and, once again, wait for the glue to dry. Alternatively, place your figure on its back, if it will lie flat, and just place the nose stone in position instead of taping it while it dries.

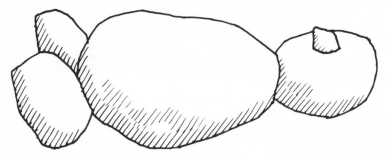

Reclining pebble person.

50

Leave the tape on your figure's nose (or leave it lying, if you didn't tape it) until the glue is dry to the touch—longer if you are nervous about its being really fixed. When you think the glue is set, peel off the tape from the nose and the foil from the bottom of the feet. Don't worry if some of the foil sticks, as long as it doesn't extend beyond the feet. If it does show, and you don't like it, you can trim off the excess foil and glue with a pair of scissors.

Unpainted Basic Pebble People—one at right also shown painted in Color Plate 7

Painting Your Pebble Person

Now you're ready to paint. As far as colors go, it really depends on what colors you like or want for the particular character your pebble person has assumed. Before you start to paint, study your pebble person from all angles. Don't start with a preconceived idea of what or who it should be. Each will assume its own personality as you stare at it or live with it. Turn it around; look for indentations and imperfections in the stones. Sometimes they suggest the character your pebble person can best become.

If your person is assembled from different color pebbles—as most will be—you'll find it best to paint the whole figure white with acrylic paint before you do any decorative painting. The white base will also make all your colors look brighter. If some of the pebbles have a rough surface, it's best to coat the figure with gesso rather than white acrylic. Gesso is much thicker than regular acrylic paints and will fill in rough spots and minor imperfections, making a smoother surface on which to paint.

1. Start with a pencil and lightly draw a few guide lines on the surface to show where the various main color areas will be—hairline, waistline, arms, hands, and so on. Now you're really ready to paint.

2. Start with the pale colors first. If your paint set doesn't have a flesh color, here's how to make it. Start with a blob of white—smaller than a dime—then add a dab of yellow ochre on the tip of your brush, and mix it with the white. When you have a pale beige, add a dab, really tiny this time, of red on the tip of your cleaned brush, and mix this in. It should now start to look something like a flesh color. If it doesn't look right, add color till it does. Make it paler than you think it should be, because it will darken a bit as it dries on your stones. Be very careful about the amount of red you use. Red is a very strong color and it doesn't take very much of it to make your pebble person's face look like a blushing beet.

3. When you are happy with the color, paint in face and hands and any other bare flesh you want, covering up your pencil guide lines as you go just enough so you don't leave any gaps when the next color goes on. You may have to repaint as it dries, especially if there are some

52

nicks in the stone that don't fill the first time. Acrylic dries quickly, and the second layer should cover just fine.

4. If you want to add color to your person's cheeks, wait for the basic skin color to dry, then mix some watery red. Put a small dab on a cheek, then immediately smear it with your finger. That will make it uneven and natural looking. Do the same thing for the other cheek, as well as the forehead, nose, or whatever you feel necessary.

5. When all the flesh is done to perfection, it's best to put in the facial features. I say to do this next because, if you want to start over, it's best to do so before you have clothes painted in that might get messed up when you paint out the face. You may find it easier to put in eyes, ears, and mouth with fine felt-tipped pens rather than a brush. And that's fine *if* you do it with waterproof colors. If you use water-soluble colors, you'll have to spray the sur-

face with artist's fixative before varnishing, or your pen lines will run. Just ask someone at your art or craft supply store if the pens you buy have waterproof or water-soluble ink.

Experiment with drawing simple faces on paper before you decide on the expression you want for your pebble person.

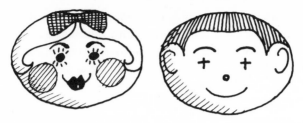

Red mouths and eyelashes tend to make pebble people look feminine. If you didn't use a nose stone, don't try to draw on a nose—just use a couple of black dots as nostrils. Babies and girls seem to look best with black-dot nostrils rather than nose stones. When you paint in hair, it's best to use an almost dry brush so the bristle lines show, leaving some base color to show through. Or paint a few irregular lines of a different shade over the first color to create the illusion of hair. Otherwise, it tends to look like

the blob of color it actually is. If you want ears on your pebble person, just paint a fine black letter *c* with the open side toward the front of the head. If you paint eyes with a lot of white showing all around the iris, your character will look surprised. If you just make slits for eyes, your pebble person will look Oriental.

Arched eyebrows, just a curved line, will also add to a surprised look. If you want an angry face, make the eyebrows come close together at the nose and lower at the nose end than at the outer end. A mouth curving down looks sad, or angry, or mean. A mouth curving up looks happy. You'll find it's fun to experiment with different

expressions for your pebble person, but the best place to do so is on a piece of paper before you start painting, or you're likely to find yourself painting layer on layer of white on your pebble person's face to paint out your mistakes.

6. Assuming that you have a face you like the look of, it's time to clothe your character. Begin with the inner layer of clothes and work toward the outer garments, ending with anything to be painted black. For example, if you have a man with shirt, tie, vest, slacks, belt, and jacket, the order of painting them on your figure should be as follows:

    1. Shirt   4. Belt
    2. Tie   5. Vest
    3. Slacks 6. Jacket

Then paint the feet (black or brown shoes if you didn't give him bare feet). Finish up with some fine-line work with black to indicate shadows, outlines, and buttons, all of which help give your pebble person a caricature look. Painting from inner garments to outer, you can paint over your guidelines and the edges of the undergarment color. No blank spots will be left if you cover the edge of each color with the subsequent paint layer.

Painted Basic Pebble
Person (see also Color
Plate 7)

A Finished Pebble Person

And here is how he may look, finished and painted, with a
beaked nose and open mouth, looking all the time as if he
had been captured in mid-sentence. The feet are two very irregular chunks of stone. They don't detract from the overall
effect because the viewer's attention is drawn more to face
and body by color. A natural bump in the stone suggested
where the left arm and the trouser pocket should be. The
slight egg shape of the body stone, placed this way up, made
a natural fat belly, accentuated by the belt buckle being
placed at the fattest point. The nose stone, almost square,
had enough curve on one corner to make a nose when placed
with the curve uppermost. The small hole that was in one
side of the head stone made a natural open mouth once a

56

red line was painted around it. The collar of his jacket at the back was formed accidentally by excess epoxy glue which squeezed out when the head stone was stuck on.

A NOTE ABOUT ARMS

If you want separate arms instead of painted ones, it's best to use a couple of flattish, long, thin stones. These are very hard to find in my experience. Glue and tape them in position, one at a time, after you have the head on. In most cases, you don't really need separate arm stones at all. The painted ones usually look every bit as natural and often more so. If you don't find stones that are just right, your figure is in danger of looking top-heavy and clumsy, especially where the

shoulders attach to the body. So take care when you decide to give your people attached arms.

There are several figures in this book with arms, some with two and some with just one. In most cases they are on larger figures, where arms seem to work out better. In some cases they are there to hold some accessory. And in one instance, I cheated a bit by smoothing out the shoulder joint with papier-mâché.

The Witch
(See also Color Plate 3)

The construction of a witch follows exactly the same steps as for the Basic Pebble Person already described, using pebbles and epoxy glue. With a witch, since a grotesque look is in character, you can use almost any rough stones—and certainly that is true of the one illustrated here.

Witch

58

The witch's grotesque nose, as you can see, adds to her witch-like quality. The shape of the head gives the character a heavy-jowled look and the broken corner of the body stone, with a coat of gesso under the finish paint to smooth it off a bit, doesn't detract from the finished figure at all. It merely makes one shoulder slope more than the other.

This is a figure with pebble arms. She needed arms to hold her broomstick. The broomstick, incidentally, is made of a twig about six inches long with its natural bark left on; shreds of cornhusk for the broom bristles are attached to the stick with a twist of thin wire. I used 24-gauge copper wire, but a small thin paperclip would probably do just fine. Her

Broomstick.

hat is a cone of paper attached to a circle of thin cardboard. They are held together with white glue and painted black. The hat was added as the last element of the figure, after everything else was completed.

HOW TO MAKE A WITCH'S HAT

1. Cut a circle of heavy white paper with a diameter twice you want your witch's hat to be high. For a 2½-inch-high hat, cut a 5-inch diameter circle.
2. Fold it in half and then in half again.

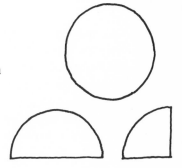

3. Cut along folds. You need one quarter section of the circle.
4. Curl the quarter circle of paper by rolling it around a pencil from the straight edges. Do this inward from both edges.

5. With your fingers, curve and shape it gently into a cone shape, with the edges of the paper just coming together at the point and over-lapping about a quarter inch at the curved edge.
6. Smear a little white glue along one of the overlapping edges and hold it together with fingers or a paper clip until the glue is set.
7. Cut a two-inch circle of heavy paper or cardboard. This will become the brim of the hat.
8. Put the cone on top of the circle and run a bead of white glue around the edge of the cone, holding down the cone with a little pressure on its top till the glue sets.

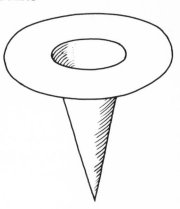

9. With a razor blade, scalpel, or craft knife, cut a circle out of the center of the brim circle big enough for the hat to sit on your witch's head.
10. Paint it black (or whatever color you want your witch's hat to be).
11. Run a bead of glue around the inner circle under the brim and set the hat on your witch's head.

The Little Girl in Red Slippers

Little Girl in Red Slippers

You'll need just four pebbles to make this charmer. The body and head stones should be fairly well-rounded specimens and quite smooth. The larger the head stone you use in proportion to the body stone, the younger your little girl will look. Just make it larger than you would use for an adult figure.

1. First assemble the four stones with epoxy, using the steps described for a Basic Pebble Person at the beginning of this chapter. Then paint the whole figure white with acrylic paint.
2. Paint face and neck, using a pinkish skin tone. To get this color, mix white with a dab of yellow ochre, then add

61

a spot of red, using slightly more red than you would for a male figure. Leave two white circles for her eyes, slightly higher than halfway up the front of the head stone.

3. Paint her hair yellow, so the red bow will show up. Alternatively, you could give her dark hair and leave a bow-shaped area of white showing through.

4. Her eyes are just spots of blue in the center of the white circles. Leaving a lot of white and adding arched black-line eyebrows adds to her air of innocence. Eyelashes are just fine black lines and nostrils two black dots. Her mouth is a cupid's-bow-shaped line of red.

5. Her blue dress rides up on one side, revealing white petticoats. The dress was painted as a solid area of pale blue, leaving white spaces where her hands would be. Hands are then painted the same color as her face.

6. Fine lines, put on with a waterproof black felt-tipped pen, outline arms and fabric creases. White collar, cuffs, and ruffles were added after the blue of her dress was dry, using thick white acrylic paint straight out of the tube.

7. The single-strap red shoes add a little-girlish touch. The purple sash around her waist turns into a big bow at the back.

8. If you used water-soluble ink to make the black lines, remember to spray

next with artist's fixative. Otherwise, she is ready for a finish coat of polymer gloss medium.

Naturally, you may want to vary colors or dress style to taste. Black for shoes instead of red would be equally appropriate, looking like black patent leather.

Man with Turban

I include him here just to show how simple a figure can be in the painting and how misshapen the pebbles can be, yet still produce a figure with lots of character. His feet are ridiculously large compared to his body and the body four times as wide front to back as it is side to side. Yet the final effect is of a cloaked figure with arms folded over his chest under the cloak. The face is left the natural brown color of the head stone and the features just three rough black lines suggesting eyes and moustache— with more black paint added unevenly with an almost dry brush for a heavy beard. The turban is a mixture of blue and white, with the suggestion of some precious stone or emblem set in a knot over his forehead.

Man with Turban

Old Lady
with Apron

You'll need seven pebbles to re-create
this figure, who has rocks for arms instead of painted on suggestions of arms.
She also has a beautiful beak-shaped
nose that could probably have made her
a very attractive witch. The character of
your old lady will be determined by the
pebbles you find and use.

Old Lady with Apron: Front
View

1. First, assemble your figure using epoxy glue as described for a Basic Pebble Person. Then add the two arm stones by gluing and taping until dry. The position in which you tape the arms will affect the look of your character, so experiment with various positions before you actually glue them on.

2. Next, paint the figure with white acrylic all over. While the paint is drying, work out the details of expression and clothing for your figure on paper, so you don't have to repaint it on the actual pebbles.

3. In making this figure, first paint face and hands with flesh tone (made from white, yellow ochre, and red, as explained for the basic pebble person). Then add hair, leaving an area of the base white coat showing to make her mobcap. Add a few crease lines in the mob cap with a black felt-tipped pen. Eyes are black dots in white circles. Eyebrows, eyelashes, and mouth are black felt-tipped pen lines.

4. Now add the clothing. First, outline the bottom of the dress and the apron, not forgetting the apron strings and bow at the back. Then paint the dress in any color you desire. You can also simulate a printed fabric by mingling dots of different colors in an allover pattern. Add folds and pockets in the apron with a felt-tipped pen. Paint the shoes.

Rear view, Old Lady with Apron.

5. If you have used water-soluble inks in the decoration of your figure, you should now spray with artist's fixative before giving your figure its final coat of polymer gloss medium.

Monk in Brown Robe
(See also Color Plate 7)

I include this figure to demonstrate that a single rock mounted on two pebbles for feet can be quite complete without separate pebbles for either head, arms, or nose. The possibility of creating such a figure depends upon the pebbles you find and what you see in them after staring at them from various directions.

To make a figure like this, you will need a stone with a head-shaped lump on one end. If the lump is off center, all the better; it will just give your figure a more inquiring look. Attach this stone with epoxy glue to two foot stones, as described in instructions for the Basic Pebble Person.

You are now ready to start painting your own version of Friar Tuck.

Monk in Brown Robe

1. First mix some flesh color paint to the flesh tone you prefer. (See instructions in Basic Pebble Person).

2. Paint the face, then paint hands where they would look most natural to you.

3. Paint the habit or robe. The one shown was painted burnt sienna brown, as was his skullcap.

4. Paint in the hair, making sure you bring the hairline down far enough, so that when you paint in the cap, there will be plenty of hair still framing the face of your figure. The monk shown has grey hair. White and black acrylic paints were mixed very slightly so that it was very streaky. This gives the effect of hair much better than painting with a solid color.

5. Paint the cap.

6. With a fine felt-tipped black pen, draw facial features. Often your rock will have indentations to which you can add a few lines to simulate expressions and features.

7. With your black pen, draw crease lines in the habit to simulate folds in the fabric, remembering to draw some lines at the top of the back of the habit to give the effect of a hood or cowl.

8. Paint a thin yellow line around the waist. You can either make this a belt or turn it into a sash by drawing more lines for the belt and adding some tassels. When the paint is dry, outline the yellow with a black pen. If you practice on paper first, you will find you will quickly become

adept at turning this thin line into a rope or a braid, depending on how you curve little lines on the yellow belt.

9. Paint shoes or sandals on the two foot stones.
10. Use artist's fixative to spray your figure if your ink is water soluble. Otherwise your figure is now ready for it's coat of ploymer gloss medium.

Happy Reveller with pencil guidelines drawn prior to painting.

The Happy Reveller
(See also Color Plate 7)

The basis of this figure is a long body stone, flat on one side, so that he looks equally effective standing up or lying flat on his back.

He is assembled by the same method as the Basic Pebble Person, using epoxy glue and masking tape. If your basic stones are dark colored, paint the whole figure with white acrylic paint or gesso first.

1. Draw a few pencil lines on the body stone to outline jacket, sleeves, and position of hands.
2. Paint face and hands in flesh color, using the technique outlined in the Basic Pebble Person instructions.
3. Paint the shirt in whatever color you

prefer. When the paint is dry, paint the jacket, then the trousers. When painting the jacket, make it a color that allows your black detail lines for lapels, pockets, and so forth, to show to advantage.

4. Using either black acrylic paint and a fine brush or a black felt-tipped pen, go over your penciled guidelines, outlining the jacket and sleeves. At this time you can add the two crosses for eyes (or simple horizontal lines to suggest closed eyes) and simple curves for mouth and eyebrows. Don't forget to add the jacket lapels, pockets, buttons, and buttonholes.

5. The hair and feet of the figure shown were painted black: the feet solid black, the hair solid at the back and ragged at the edges. This fellow took on a very sorry look when a dab of pink was added to the end of his nose to make him look slightly inebriated. What expression you add to your figure is your choice. Once you have given your particular reveller his expression, he will only need his protective coat of gloss polymer medium. (Remember—artist's fixative before the polymer medium coat if you have used water-soluble inks).

Happy Reveller: Painted

69

The Caveman

(See also Color Plate 10)

This aggressive-looking chap is clad in a piece of fur fabric to simulate an animal skin. It was attached with white glue after the figure was all assembled. He is made from six pebbles, with just one arm to hold his sharpened stake. You don't really notice the fact that one arm is missing. It could be under his animal skin coat. This figure shows how much latitude there is in this craft for departing from nature or realism and still getting a good effect. Now here's how to make him.

Caveman: Front View

1. Gather your six pebbles. The size of the pebbles will depend on what you have available. The body stone should be squarish with, of course, rounded corners. The head stone should be egg shaped and attached to the body by one of the long sides to add to the Neanderthal effect. Foot

70

stones should be large and flat. The arm should be long and the nose a squarish chip.

2. Assemble your caveman in the same manner as other figures, then paint him all over with a dark flesh tone— darker than most other characters in this book because, after all, cavemen spent a lot of time outdoors getting weather-beaten. Add raw sienna to your white and yellow ochre paint to achieve this. Paint on hair using dark brown or black, making it very ragged around the edges. His eyes should just peep out from behind this matted hair and, since cave men rarely shaved, paint on a beard on the lower half of his face, leaving a spot for a red slash of a mouth. Since your cave man wouldn't be likely to have shoes, paint his feet the same color as his body and suggest toes with a few black lines. Then give the whole figure a coat of polymer gloss medium.

3. Now make his animal skin coat, using a piece of fur fabric. Measure him around the middle and cut a rectangle of fur fabric about a half inch wider than this measurement and as deep as his body height from shoulder to feet. Now cut an oval hole in one side of your fabric strip to go over his arm. Then cut a piece off each top corner diagonally, and a curve out of the bottom opposite the oval hole, as shown in the illustration. This is to

A = Caveman's height, shoulder to feet.

B = Distance around fattest part of caveman, plus ½" for overlap.

C = Space for caveman's arm

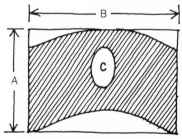

Approximate shape for cutting fur fabric.

leave his other shoulder bare. Now slip his arm through the hole and wrap the fur fabric around his body to see how it fits. Trim it as necessary to look the way you want it, leaving enough fabric for a slight overlap.

4. Remove the fabric from your caveman when you are satisfied with the fit and, with white glue, apply glue to the back of the fur fabric around the arm hole and along the top and side edges, as shown in the shaded areas of this illustration. Of course, after you've trimmed the fur fabric to fit your particular caveman's body, it probably won't be as even a shape as in this illustration, but this will give you the general idea.

5. Now slip the arm hole over his arm and wrap the fur fabric around, making sure it sticks down smoothly around the arm and shoulder and where it overlaps. Leave it unglued at the bottom, hanging naturally close to the feet front and back and up higher at the arm side to expose one foot and part of the body stone beneath the arm. You may also have to clip and overlap some edges to make the fur fit around the body, depending upon the shape of the stone and the amount of stretch in your fur fabric.

6. When the glue is dry, clip the pile of the fabric unevenly with scissors to give it the worn, moth-eaten look that befits the garb of a hard-living caveman.

7. Make his spear from any scrap of wood. A piece of balsa is good because it can be easily scraped and shaped with a kitchen knife or pocket knife to look like a rough stake. Whatever you use, make the spear rough finished. You don't want it to look as though it had been turned out on a twentieth-century lathe. Sharpen it at one end and paint it a mixture of brown and grey to give it a weather-beaten look. A red tip will add a touch of gory realism.

8. Attach the spear with a spot of epoxy glue to toe and hand.

Side View

The Two Farmers

(See also Color Plate 4)

THE SETTING

1. The first step in making this twosome is to find a fairly large flattish rock for a base. The base shown is a piece of granite about six inches long, three inches wide, and about an inch thick. The size of the rock you use is determined by the size of the figures you intend to put on it. The figures shown here are nearly three inches high, so judge your composition accordingly.

Two Farmers

2. Now build the fence. The split-rail
   fence is made of balsa because it's
   easy to work with. Balsa is easily obtained in craft supply stores, where
   you can either get a single piece or
   better yet a bundle of assorted scrap
   pieces. The posts shown are about a
   half inch square and an inch and a
   half long. The rails are about a
   quarter inch square and three inches
   long. You will need to adjust these
   sizes to fit the size of your grouping.
       Balsa cuts very easily but also splits
   easily, so when cutting rails or posts
   from a sheet of balsa, use a metal
   straightedge or ruler. With a craft
   knife or razor blade, make a number

of light cuts rather than one heavy
one to cut out your pieces.

3. After cutting out your pieces, scrape
them so that they look rough and uneven. The ends of each rail should be
pared down to about half the
thickness of the rest of the rail where
they will go through the upright posts,
starting about three-fourths of an inch
from the end as shown.

Shape of rail.

4. Bore a hole through the upright posts
to take the end of the rails (they will
overlap on the center post). Holes
can be drilled with an electric drill if
you have a variable-speed drill and
use the slowest speed. A high-speed
drill will probably split the posts. Easier, if slower, is to bore the holes with
a small screwdriver, turning and
pressing slowly until you get through.
You can also do it with the point of a
small pocket knife or craft knife, using
the same twisting motion. If you do
accidentally split a post while boring a
hole, don't throw it away. Just cut
half a hole in each of the split pieces
and glue them back together again
with white glue. When it is painted,
you'll never know it was split.

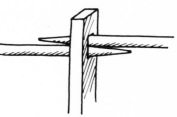

Rails overlapping
through post.

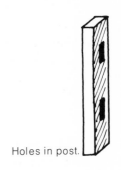

Holes in post.

5. Assemble the fence with white glue
into a unit. Then fix it to the base
rock with epoxy glue at the bottom of
each post. Hold the posts in position

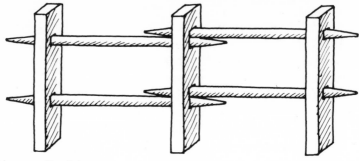

How a split-rail fence
should be assembled.

by taping them over the top of each
post and down to the sides of the
rock until the epoxy is dry. When the
epoxy is set, paint the fence grey, the
weather-beaten color of an old split-
rail cedar fence.

THE PEOPLE

1. With the fence in position, build the
   pebble people where you want them,
   on the base and against the rails. First
   glue the feet down. Then glue the
   bodies to the feet, leaning them
   against the fence rail so that they can
   set in position. The heads come next.
   Glue and tape them to the bodies.
   Lastly, add a single arm to each figure, just touching the fence, to add to
   the conversational look. Tape the
   arms to bodies and fence until the
   epoxy dries.
2. In painting the figures, you will need

76

to take care to avoid spattering the fence rails. Colors and dress will be your choice. A bib-and-brace overall such as the one worn by one of the figures shown helps create a rural atmosphere. Also, since they are supposedly conversing, at least one figure should have an open mouth as though in mid-sentence. If you give them both open mouths, it will appear they are having an argument. The rock base should have its top painted irregularly with green to suggest grass. Any green will do, but the color called Hooker's Green will give you the best grass color. Coat just the figures with polymer gloss medium, to give contrast to the grass and the weather-beaten fence.

Note: The figures can be constructed separately, then glued in position after they are painted. This makes painting the figures easier, but it also makes it more difficult to work out the exact angles for each stone in relation to the fence.

Baseball Player

Six pebbles will make this old-time slugger, plus a piece of aluminum foil for his cap and a whittled-down piece of balsa for his bat. The project is completed with an irregularly-shaped piece of cardboard painted green, white, and sandy brown to suggest home plate. A nice flat rock would make an even better base. The steps in making this baseball player are essentially like those for any pebble person.

1. Assemble feet, body, head, nose, and arm with epoxy glue and tape.
2. Give the whole figure a coat of gesso to make an evenly colored base on which you can then paint his features and uniform. Paint his head complete with hair even though you'll give him a cap later, because some hair will show under it.
3. Whittle down a piece of balsa to the shape of a bat and attach it with epoxy glue to the hand and shoulder of the figure.
4. Make his cap from a small piece of household aluminum foil. Fold in the edges until you get a round shape with a squarish peak on one side.

Baseball Player: Back View

Foil for cap.

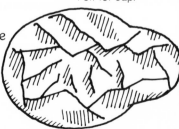

78

Then mold it over your slugger's head to his particular cranium shape by squeezing down the sides. Foil shapes very easily. When you are satisfied with the look and angle of the cap, glue it to the head with epoxy, then paint it to match his uniform.

5. Now finish the whole figure, including the bat, with gloss polymer medium. You may need to give the bat several coats to make it shine, since balsa wood is very absorbent.

Rear view, Baseball Player.

The Accountant

Accountant

This cigar-chewing chap is slightly more complicated than some other constructions, but the fun of making him is well worth the effort. Start with the standard steps of making a pebble person—feet, body, head, nose, arms last. Then add some non-pebble accessories. The accountant shown here carries a calculator, is smoking a fat cigar, and has a pencil sticking in his hair. Your pebble person

could just as easily be a doctor, lawyer,
or Indian chief. It all depends on what
accessories you decide to add to the
basic figure.

The calculator and cigar are both
made of balsa, whittled to shape and attached to the figure with epoxy glue. The
curly hair, eyebrows, and moustache are
made from papier-mâché. I used the
ready-made, powdered kind that you
can buy in art and craft supply stores. It
is inexpensive, convenient, and easy to
use.

To put the character together, you do
the following:

1. Assemble the basic figure as pre-
   viously explained, selecting a thin or
   fat body stone depending on the kind
   of pebble person you want. The arm
   holding the calculator should point
   downward.
2. Whittle a small block of balsa to the
   shape of a calculator in proportion to
   the size of the figure you are making.
   While you are working with the balsa,
   make a tiny cigar.
3. For the hair, smooth a lump of papier-mâché around his head. When
   the basic shape satisfies you, give it
   the texture you want. For curly hair
   you can poke it all over with the point
   of a pencil. For straight hair, try using
   a needle tip to draw lines. The commercial papier-mâché dries overnight
   and needs no glue other than the
   paste in the compound itself to make

it stick to your stone. If you want to speed up the drying process, you can also put your rock, with the commercial papier-mâché on it, in a warm oven (set at about 175° Fahrenheit) until it hardens.

4. Attach the calculator to the hand and the cigar to the mouth with epoxy glue.

5. Now paint the figure, first the flesh, then the hair. When painting over the papier-mâché, thin your paint more than usual so you get good coverage. Paint in the clothes.

6. Now you can add the pencil, which is a small piece of balsa painted yellow with a grey end and black tip. Make a small hole in the hair with a nail or pencil point and stick the pencil in. Finish your pebble person with a coat of polymer gloss medium.

The Scarred Pugilists

These two battered faces seemed natural for the two rough, flat stones that I used. I just added two small stones for noses.

1. Lay your flat stones on your working surface, making sure they are steady, and attach the nose stones with epoxy glue.
2. Paint the stones with gesso to smooth the surface, then add the features, bandages, and any other embellishments you want.
3. Give the faces a coat of polymer gloss medium and while it is drying make a simple shadow box to accommodate the faces. Paint the box with acrylic paint and leave it to dry.

4. Stick the faces in the shadow box
   with epoxy glue.

Note: This project could be made entirely
with white glue, although it would take
longer. It would then be a safe and
enjoyable project for children.

Conversations

The scarred pugilists described in the
previous project are one way of making
a picture with pebbles. Here is a more
sophisticated concept, using natural colored, unpainted stones, where the picture depends on the design and arrangement of the pebbles themselves rather
than their decoration. Such pictures are
fun to make if you have a source of suitable stones available to you.

To make one, you need flat, well
smoothed stones of various shapes and,
preferably, all the same color. The best
source for such stones in their natural
state is a river bed rather than the seashore, although there are some beaches
where stones of one color are predominant. The pebbles in this picture came
from Vermont and are probably slate

84

chips well worn by the fast-running
mountain stream I found them in.

When you have collected a bunch of
such stones, sort them into three cat-
egories: small oval or elongated ones
which will be useful for feet and arms;
large oval or elongated ones which will
become bodies; and round or close-to-
round shapes which will make good
heads. Then start assembling figures,
with or without arms, on any flat surface.
From individual figures, go on to pairs
and groups of figures making and re-
making your arrangements in different
ways. Don't be satisfied with the first arrangement you devise. There are
hundreds of ways in which both pebbles
and resulting figures might be put
together to make a picture. If any particular arrangement looks great, but you
want to try others, it's easy to make a
quick sketch of the groupings before you
take them apart, so that you can go back
to it any time you want. When you are

satisfied that you have the best possible
arrangement, you are ready to turn it
into a picture. Here's how:

1. First look for some background material that contrasts with your pebbles,
   or at least makes them stand out
   nicely. The picture shown at the
   beginning of this project uses a piece
   of light-colored grass cloth, against
   which the gray of the pebbles shows
   up well. But a painted background,
   art-papers, colored construction
   paper, wallpaper, natural or stained
   wood may be best for your stones.
   So, if your stones are light colored,
   choose a dark background; if they are
   dark, get a light background; if the
   stones are mottled in color, make
   sure the background is plain. Con-
   versely, if the stones are plain, you
   can make use of a patterned background. Again, the secret is to experiment with several different materials
   to see which looks best.
2. Next, make your frame. If your picture is to hang on the wall, you'll
   need a wooden frame or a shadow
   box strong enough to support the
   weight of your pebbles. What sort of
   frame you use is up to you. A
   shadow box made of flat strips or
   planks of wood is easiest to make,
   but a purchased frame (look in the
   attic or the local junk shop) without
   glass and deep enough so your pebbles don't protrude beyond the plane

of the front of your frame, will do fine. However, once you have selected your frame, and before you do anything else, remove backing, picture and glass from it, lay it flat on a sheet of paper, face up, and draw a line around the inside edge. This will give you a shape on which to make your final pebble arrangement prior to glueing them in position.

3. Now cut a backboard from a piece of ¼'' plywood or pegboard, to fit the outside dimension of your frame. Cover the front of this backboard with whatever surface material you have chosen as contrasty enough, by glueing it solidly all over. Remember, it has to bear the weight of your stones, so it mustn't slip or pull off the backboard.

4. Glue and nail your covered backboard to the back of your picture frame or shadow box, and smooth off the edges when the glue is set. Do any touch-up staining, painting, or polishing that may be necessary to the outside of the frame at this stage. It's easier than when you have the pebbles glued in.

5. Now you're ready to mount your stones. But first, arrange your pebbles within the pencil on paper outline you drew in step 2, to make sure they still look right, or to make any last minute adjustments. Now transfer stones to finished shadow box frame.

6. This is best done by moving the fig-

ure nearest the center of your arrangement first—pebble by pebble. A
couple of spots of epoxy on each
should be sufficient. Or, if you're in
no hurry, and can leave your picture
flat overnight, white glue will do the
job. After the center figure, transfer
and fix the two closest to the outer
edges and then fill in those in between. Finish by varnishing the
stones with polymer gloss medium if
you want them to look shiny. If not,
the picture is finished and ready to
hang once you have nailed a saw-
tooth hanger to the back or provided
some other means of support.

Note: If you want to make a pebble
picture and can't find stones all of the
same color, you can of course paint
them all one color before you glue pebbles into a frame. You can also decorate
them with colors in the same way as
three-dimensional pebble people, to add
clothes and facial features. Then again,
you may just make an attractive arrangement with a group of mixed color or texture pebbles, which is abstract rather
than relying on animal or human forms.

Popeyed Penguin (see also p. 122)

Bottom Row: Two Fishy Friends (see also p. 33)
Worm (see also p. 40);
Top Row: Mexican Design (see also p. 32) Fishy Friend;
Lovable Ladybug (see also p. 35);

Ogling Owl (see also p. 36);   Witch (see also p. 58)
Owl with Glasses (see also p. 111);

Wire and Rock Tree (see also page 165); Two Farmers (see also page 73)

Chirpy Chicks (see also p. 39)

Three-Headed Zany (see also p. 38)

Left to Right: Monk in Brown Robe (see also p. 66); Happy Reveller (see also p. 68); Basic Pebble Person (see also p. 46)

Left: One-Color Design
Right: Little Brown Wren (outlined in indelible black felt-tip, filled in with acrylic; courtesy Evelyn L. Brannon)

Paperweight (see also p. 131) Découpaged Rock (see also p. 29);

Furry Hedgehog (see also p. 138) Caveman (see also p. 70);

Left to Right: Spotted Spiny Alligator (see also p. 148); Ginger the Cat (see also p. 118); Deep Sea Fish (see also p. 108)

Love-Sick Lady Whale (see also p. 42)

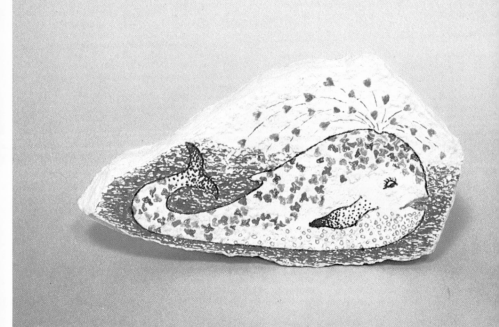

ANIMAL
FRIENDS

Pebble groups don't have to become people. Some stones just naturally suggest animal forms from the moment you pick them up. Animals are fun to make, so let's look at the steps and some of the difficulties that are part of creating them.

You may find you enjoy making animals even more than making rock people because you can introduce a greater degree of fantasy. People, to look at all like people, have to have some recognizable features, but who knows what strange forms animals have taken since the dawn of creation? And you may unknowingly be duplicating some as-yet-undiscovered prehistoric monster. The fact is that you can do just about anything when it comes to making rock animals— multiple heads, wings, horns, and feelers are all part of the fun. They all make for a more fantastic creature.

97

Like people, animals don't have to be multi-rock creations. You may find a single stone some day that's flat enough on one side to just lie there and end up looking like some animal or other. After all, most four-legged animals lie down from time to time, and they they're just a fat bulk of one shape or another. And if you find a rock that has the makings of a head at one end, you're in business with a single-rock animal—like some of the suggestions at the end of chapter 1. I had a beautiful rock dog that arrived complete with head and body all in one stone. All it needed was a coat of paint to turn it into a long-haired sheep dog.

If you want your animal to be more or less normal—with four legs, a neck, one head, a tail, and so on—here's how to go about making it. To show you step-by-step, we'll start off by making what is supposed to be a dog.

BASIC DOG

1. Assemble all the pebbles you think you'll need. For a dog like the one shown here, you'll want a long body stone, a neck stone, the head stone, four leg stones and some little chips of stone for nose, eyes, and ears. The tail can be a stone if you find one you like, or it can just as easily be a piece of string. The basic stones I used are shown here.

Pebbles for Basic Dog

98

The biggest problem you're likely to have is finding four legs that are more or less about the same dimensions. They don't have to be exact. If you can't find four all alike, you can match them in pairs, with one pair longer than the other. This will mean that the animal's body will be at a different angle in relation to the ground than that shown here. He may look as though he is squatting or leaping, depending upon how you attach the two pairs of leg stones. The legs don't have to be particularly smooth or round. You'll find when you are all through painting that the focus of attention tends to be on the head of your fantasy friend. The legs become just incidental supports.

2. The first putting together to do with any animal character is to attach the legs, if it is in fact to have legs. First, turn the body upside down or lay it on its back. Decide where the four corners of your animal's body are. Attach three of the legs in three of the corners, one at a time, by putting a blob of epoxy glue on the end of the leg and taping it into the position you want with masking tape.

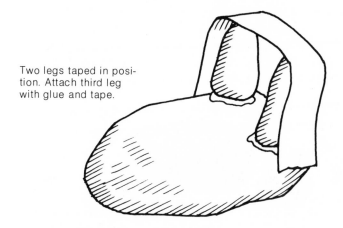

Two legs taped in position. Attach third leg with glue and tape.

When these three legs are set and the glue is dry, turn your animal right side up. You will find that it will stand up on its three legs quite nicely. In this, it's just like any tripod or a three-legged stool that will always stand firmly on three legs even if they are all of dissimilar length. Don't try to attach the fourth leg in the same way that you did the first three, with the body upside down. Instead, have your headless creation stand on his three good legs. Take the fourth leg and find a place on the remaining corner of his body where the leg will touch both body and ground at the same time and look best. You'll probably have to turn the leg around a few times to find the place where it fits best. Don't worry about its not fitting right under the body stone or about its being a bit too close to one of the others or sticking out sideways at a slightly different angle than the other three. After all, dogs often do stick out a leg for reasons best known to them.

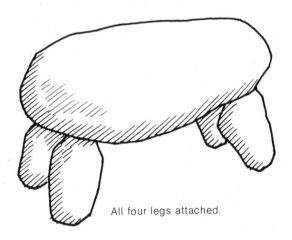

All four legs attached.

When you're happy with the position, put some epoxy glue on top of this spare leg and place it in the position you chose, propping it there if necessary with cans, stones, or anything handy until the glue is set. Don't be impatient if you don't think you've got enough glue on to hold the leg. It needs surprisingly little epoxy to hold a leg firm. When it's set, you can always turn the body upside

100

down again and add some more glue, if you feel it needs strengthening.

3. With the dog the right way up, standing on his four legs, attach neck and tail with epoxy glue, holding them in position with masking tape. If you want a curly tail, a piece of pipe cleaner or wire is useful. I've even used a small spring on occasion. If you decide on a wire tail, shape it first and make a flat coil on the end that will attach to the body. The flat coil will give the epoxy something to set in and around, thus making a firm joint. It's best also to make sure that the glue is under and over the coil for extra strength. When gluing any metal to stone, it helps to roughen the part where the glue will go with a nail file or something. This gives the glue a better chance of holding. The roughening won't show when you're finished, because it will be covered with glue and paint.

Assembled dog with coil tail.

4. When the neck is dry (and in this case, give it a little longer than five minutes to make sure it's hard enough, so

101

it won't sag when you put a head on it) you're ready to proceed. You could, of course, attach ears, eyes, and nose to the head before attaching head to neck. For the dog shown, I attached ears and nose to the head while waiting for the legs to dry, but it's usually best to wait until the head is on. The particular angle at which the head stone is finally attached is often a guide to the best place to put the features to get the most expressive face. Attach the head to the neck about three quarters of the way along the head stone, with the smaller part sticking out the back and the larger part out front. Then tape it in position while the epoxy dries.

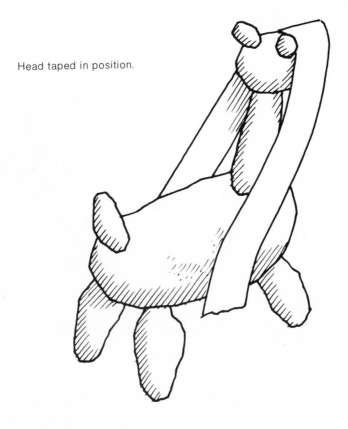

Head taped in position.

ANIMAL FRIENDS

Assembled dog with face stones attached.

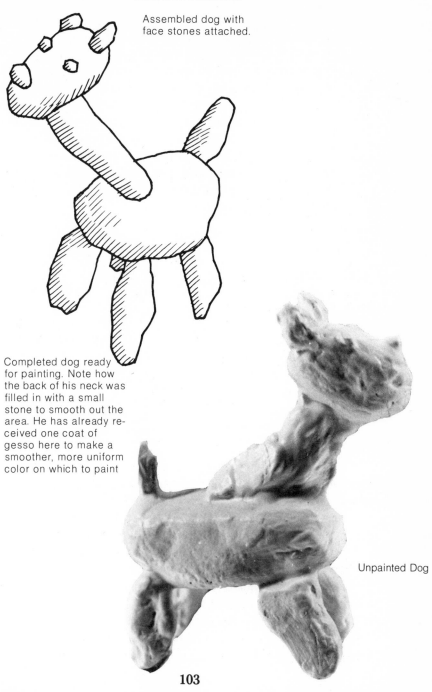

Completed dog ready for painting. Note how the back of his neck was filled in with a small stone to smooth out the area. He has already received one coat of gesso here to make a smoother, more uniform color on which to paint

Unpainted Dog

Now for details: a round or oval nose on top of the front of the head and two round or almost round eyes wherever you want to place them. If you can't find tiny pebbles just right for these features, little beads are just fine. When they are painted over you'll never know the difference. For ears, if you want them, select pebbles the size you want the ears to be. Shards of broken glass make quite good ears, but can be lethal to fingers. If you do use bits of glass, run a blob of epoxy along the sharp edges after you've attached them to the head. It dries clear and smooth and makes for greater peace of mind when friends start to examine your creations.

Left: Two long pebbles for ears; two tiny pebbles for eyes and another for nose. Right: Two pieces of felt for ears, attached with white glue.

Another way of handling glass before you attach it to your stones is to rub down the sharp edges on wet-grade emery paper, the sort used in bottle-cutting kits. You can get it in most craft supply and many hardware stores. To use it, lay the emery paper flat on the bottom of your kitchen sink and run in enough water to keep the emery surface covered while you work. Then rub the sharp edges of the glass back and forth on the emery paper until it is smoothed off enough to be safe.

As with all the other elements, each facial feature is glued and taped in position until dry. You can usually manage to tape both eyes at the same time, and perhaps

Basic Dog

the nose too with a second piece of tape, but you'll probably have to tape the ears separately.

5. If the stones used in the assembly of your dog are of different colors, you'll find it best to paint the whole assembly white with either gesso or acrylic paint before you go on to the final decoration. That way, you'll make a smoother surface to paint on because you'll fill in a lot of the little holes and cracks in the pebble surfaces. And your colors will be lighter, brighter, and more even put on over a white base coat. There's nothing wrong with using white acrylic house paint at this stage, if you have some left over. Whatever you do, don't start in on the final decorative painting until you've looked him over from all angles or lived with him long enough for his own innate personality to emerge.

105

Finned Fishes

Finned Fishes

Both of the fish shown are made of two pebbles, one for the body and the other for the base. Body and base are attached to each other with epoxy glue. The fins are cut from scraps of felt and attached with white glue. The long, fierce-looking fellow looked a bit sharkish in his unpainted form, so that is what he became with the help of black and white paint. Since those particular stones were rather rough, two coats of gesso were necessary to smooth them out after the fish was mounted on its base. The eyes and mouth both fell in natural indentations in the stone. He was a bit on the lumpy side overall, but this didn't hurt the finished look. It did, however, determine the irregular drawing of the scales, which was done using a felt-tipped pen with waterproof ink.

The happier looking fish, with open eyes, is painted directly on the pebble without any base coat. The stone happened to be an attractive light color and smooth, so no base coat was needed. The scales were made with a checkerboard of lines. There is a spot of white paint in each square formed by the lines.

To make a finned fish, do the following:

1. Take your two basic pebbles (one for the fish, one for the base) and attach them with epoxy glue.
2. If the pebbles are rough or of a color that would detract from the colors you wish to paint the fish, paint the whole thing, fish and base, with a coat of gesso.
3. Pencil in your fish scales design. These don't have to look like real fish scales; you can let your imagination run wild.
4. Paint in the facial features. If there are any indentations in the pebbles you are using, try to utilize them for the features. This often adds character and gives the illusion of bringing the pebble creatures to life.
5. Cut tiny fins for the sides from scraps of felt. The shape of the fins will be determined by the shape of the pebbles you are working with.
6. Attach the fins to the fish with white glue. Try to use a very fine line of white glue, but don't worry if some gets on the design. White glue dries

clear. You will have to attach one fin at a time, with the fish supported in such a way that you can stand the fin upright while the glue sets. If you don't use too much glue, this won't take very long.

7. Apply finish to the fish, being careful not to get any polymer medium on the felt fins.

The Deep Sea Fish

(See also Color Plate 11)

Deep Sea Fish

Here, the basic fish rock is again glued to another base rock. Copper wire, four beads (old or new), and some felt scraps are used for decoration.

1. Make the antenna first. Start with a single strand of very thin copper wire—I used 24-gauge bought at a hardware store. Stand your fish and base on the table, then measure from the table up and across the fish's back and down the other side to the table again. Add an inch and a half to this measurement. Cut your wire to this size. Make a loop about an eighth of an inch long on one end. Slip the two small beads onto the wire. Make another loop of the same size at the

108

other end to keep them from coming off. Squeeze the loops flat. Put a blob of epoxy at the ends to fix the beads in position. When they are fixed, make four folds, each three-quarters of an inch wide, in the center of the wire, as shown. These are to hold the epoxy where the antenna is glued to the fish's back.

Folded wire.

Now glue the antenna across the fish's back about level with where the eyes are to go. Put epoxy under and over the zigzag part of the copper wire. With the antenna bent downward as shown, the ends should touch the table and help hold the wire in position while the glue sets. Put a small piece of aluminum foil on top of the zigzag part of the wire while the epoxy is wet. This is to cover the ridges of the wire and prevent them from showing when the fish is painted. When the glue is dry, bend the antenna ends upward into curves to the position you can see on the finished fish.

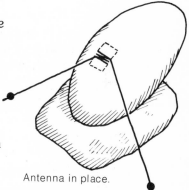

Antenna in place.

2. For eyes, use the two larger beads. Glue them on with epoxy and tape them until they set.

3. Paint the body white if you wish.

Unpainted Deep Sea Fish

Leave the base its natural color if you like, to be finished later.

4. Cut a tail fin from a piece of felt and stick it on with white glue, being careful to use just a fine line of glue.

5. Paint a design on your fish. Use the brightest acrylic color you can find, because this is a tropical fish, and tropical fish are renowned for their bright, bold colors.

6. Add a back fin cut from felt. Again, attach it with white glue.

7. Give the whole fish a coat of polymer gloss medium, being careful not to get the finish on the felt fins and tail.

110

Owl with Glasses

(See also Color Plate 3)

Owl with Glasses

This wise old character is made of just two pebbles, one for his body and one for his beak. He stands on an epoxy foot. To make an owl like this one, proceed as follows:

1. First, make the epoxy foot. Mix a blob of epoxy, rather more than you would make up for attaching two pebbles together. Place this blob of epoxy on a piece of aluminum foil. Take the pebble that is going to be the owl's body and place it firmly in the epoxy. Support the pebble with a paint jar or some such thing until the glue is set hard. Then, peel or trim off the excess foil so it doesn't show.
2. Attach a tiny sliver of stone for the beak with epoxy glue.
3. Paint eyes on either side of the beak—big circles. I used a mixture of white and yellow acrylic paint.
4. Paint his beak—I used yellow ochre and orange—and then his body. The owl shown has a dabbed-on mixture of raw sienna, burnt sienna, and burnt umber on the natural stone, which was a beige color. There is no need to try to achieve total coverage when painting the body. If you leave

111

some of the basic rock color showing through, you will get a dappled effect which will simulate feathers.

5. Outline the eyes in black and add black-dot pupils.

6. Make eyeglasses from a piece of 24-gauge copper wire wound into two loops around the end of a pencil. You could also use a thin paper clip to make the glasses. Glue these to the owl's nose with epoxy glue. Try to attach the bridge of the glasses at the point where the nose is attached to the rock, that is, at the bridge of the nose. This will give added strength.

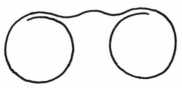

How thin copper wire should be bent to form owl's spectacles.

U-shaped lines simulating feathers.

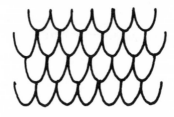

7. Finish the whole owl with a coat of polymer gloss medium. If you feel it is necessary, attach a small piece of felt to the bottom of the epoxy foot using white glue.

Four different simple treatments for your owl's eyes.

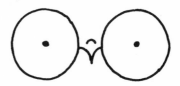

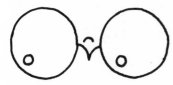

Star·Studded Giraffe

Star-Studded Giraffe

This friendly giraffe was constructed in exactly the same way as the dog, except that the giraffe has a much longer neck stone. You'll notice that the legs are not smooth at all. In fact, they were granite chips picked up on a road. But it didn't matter at all by the time he was assembled and painted.

114

The construction of this friendly giraffe is basically the same as for a dog or any other four-legged creature. But there are a few differences to consider. So if you want to make one, here's how to go about it. And, as you can see from this photo, you can use really rough and odd shaped stones for legs (these are granite chips from a road construction site) and still end up with a cute creation.

1. Start with a body stone and four leg stones. For a giraffe, remember that the body is relatively short—compared to most other quadrapeds, that is—and the legs appear to be rather close together. In fact with a real giraffe, it's difficult to say where body ends and legs or neck begin. Anyway, start with a body stone only about one and a half times as long as it is wide.

2. Attach the four legs in the same way as for a dog. If you haven't made a dog yet, turn back to that project and read how to attach four legs so your animal stands on them all without rocking or wobbling. There's a minor difference though. Make your giraffe's legs splay outwards a bit when you attach them, rather than having them completely vertical. That will offset any tendency to tip from the weight of a long neck and head.

3. Now attach your giraffe's neck. You'll need a long neck stone. If you can get one that's fatter at one end than

the other and shaped so that the fat end can be attached to the body stone at a good angle, you'll get a more realistic looking effect. But, as you can see from our giraffe, that's not an essential. It does need to be long though. Our giraffe's neck is just about as long as legs and body combined. It could be even longer than that, but not so long that it becomes top-heavy. Glue it on with epoxy, and tape it in position. Make sure the epoxy is set hard before you attach the head, or the neck may sag from its weight.

4. Attach a head stone to the top of the neck. This should be sort of oval-shaped, preferably bigger at one end than the other, and attached with the larger end toward the rear, so the smaller end can become your giraffe's mouth and nose end.

5. Ears, eyes, and nose on this giraffe are small chips of stone glued and taped in position. Adult giraffes also have little stumpy horns on top of their heads and between the ears, which you might want to add to your giraffe. There wasn't enough room on this one's head—so it became a hornless baby giraffe.

6. The tail can be added while the ears, eyes, and so forth are setting. Giraffes' tails actually hang down like a rope with a tassel on the end. You can of course make such a tail with a piece of string with a knot near the

end, and the rope beyond the knot frayed or unravelled to give it a tassel look. I wanted a perky look, so added a rock-tail pointing upward.

7. If you want your giraffe to look like the real thing, paint him white all over first, then add irregularly shaped patches of sandy-brown color with white lines in between. His underside and bottom of legs should stay white, except for his hooves. If you don't care about realism, of course, you can paint him any color or design that pleases you.

Realistic painting of giraffe

Ginger
the Cat
(See also Color Plate 11)

Ginger the Cat

To make this character you will need a total of seven stones: a body stone, a head stone, two ears, a nose, and two foot stones. You will also need a small piece of curved aluminum wire for a tail and two pieces of thin copper wire for whiskers, 24-gauge or thinner.

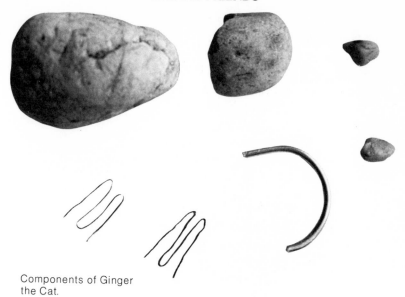

Components of Ginger
the Cat.

1. Fix the aluminum wire tail to the
   body stone with epoxy glue. Arrange
   it so that the tail curves round to the
   front of the body stone. The body
   stone will stand inside the loop of
   wire, the tip of the tail just meeting
   the epoxied end at the back.
   Roughen the wire where it will touch
   the body. Place it on a piece of aluminum foil as a working base to hold
   the epoxy glue. Use a liberal blob of
   epoxy inside and on the wire before
   sitting the body stone in position. The
   stone may stand in position without
   any support. If not, prop it with other
   stones or jars, as you would a pebble
   person body.

2. While the body and tail are drying in position make whiskers from the copper wire. You need two pieces of wire, each about four inches long. Fold these concertina fashion, so that you will have a set of four whiskers for each side of your cat's mouth. Lay the head stone face up on your working table and attach the whiskers to either side of the cat's mouth. Support the unglued ends of the whiskers so that they don't slide. It's best to put epoxy both under and on top of the whiskers to make sure that they don't fall off later. Don't cut the loops until the epoxy is set hard. You can easily cut the loops later with scissors so that you have four straight whiskers which you can then adjust to any angle pleasing to you.

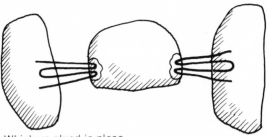

Whiskers glued in place and supported.

3. Attach the ear stones to the head stone, using epoxy glue and tape.

Ears glued and taped in position.

120

4. Attach the head stone to the body with epoxy and masking tape. Add a couple of chips (your foot stones) for front paws. Since your cat is self-supporting on tail and body, the paws won't need taping. Just set your cat on a piece of aluminum foil, place the feet in position, and add a dab of epoxy. It will run between feet and body to hold them.

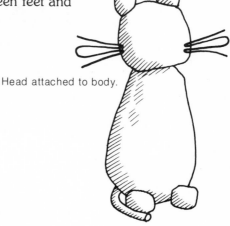

Head attached to body.

5. Add the nose stone with epoxy and tape. Or, as with the happy reveller in chapter 3, lay your cat flat on his back so that the nose stone will set in position without taping.

Nose in place.

121

6. Paint your cat all over with a coat of gesso or white acrylic paint. When this is dry, paint any color you wish. The cat shown is reddish brown with a white front painted halfway up the body, a pink blob of a nose, white lined ears, two white front paws and short black lines drawn on to simulate tiger markings.
7. Give the cat a finish coat of polymer gloss medium.

Popeyed Penguin

(See also Color Plate 1)

Many rocks seem to be naturally penguin shaped. When you find one, hunt for two small stones for feet and another small stone for a nose. Buy a card of plastic bubble buttons, carried in most fabric stores (they come in various sizes). When you have collected these few things, you can make a Popeyed Penguin.

1. Attach the body stone to the feet with epoxy glue as you would if you were making a pebble person. When the epoxy is dry, lay your penguin on his back and attach his nose with epoxy. Tape it in position and leave to dry.

122

2. If your plastic buttons have shanks, you can cut the shanks off quite easily with scissors. Attach the eye buttons to the penguin's head with epoxy and tape.
3. Paint the penguin all over with gesso or white acrylic paint and leave to dry.
4. With a pencil line, mark off the black part of your penguin and paint it black.
5. Give the penguin its finish coat of polymer gloss medium.

Popeyed Penguin

The Circus Rider

This is a more complicated piece. It consists of two figures, the horse and its rider, put together. The horse was made first and completed by the same process as the dog. The rider was assembled separately, with the exception of his feet, which were glued in position on the back of the horse just in front of the tail. Thus the top of the tail and feet made a natural three-sided support into which the footless rider was easily glued. Masking tape supported the rider until the glue set. The reins were a loop of elastic band stuck on with epoxy glue after the whole assemblage had been painted and finished.

If you want toes or hooves on your horse, collect several tiny pebbles or shards of rock. For toes, place your animal on a piece of aluminum foil and glue your pebbles or shards around the bottom of the legs. If you want to achieve the look of a one-piece hoof, take a piece of aluminum wire, hammer it flat, and make a loop. Cut it to the size you want and attach it around the bottom of each leg with the open end of the loop toward the back. Aluminum wire will bend and shape easily with your fingers. You can also shape it around a pencil or some similar article.

Circus Rider

The Fantailed Duck

The original shape of the stone dictated
that it should become a duck's body.
The head and feet were attached in the
usual way with epoxy glue. The fantail
was made as a separate unit out of four
toothpicks and attached to the duck as a
complete unit.

Fantailed Duck

HOW TO MAKE A TOOTHPICK FAN-
TAIL

1. Cut two toothpicks almost in half. Cut
   two others slightly more off center so
   that you end up with four pairs of
   slightly varying lengths.

126

2. Arrange them symmetrically on a piece of aluminum foil, placing the longest pieces in the middle and the shortest on the outside.

3. Arrange them into a fan shape with the cut ends touching, the pointed ends spread. Put a blob of epoxy glue on the ends that are touching. Reposition if necessary to get the effect you want.

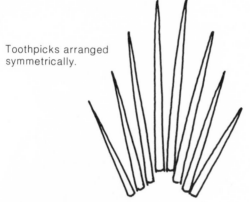

Toothpicks arranged symmetrically.

4. When the glue is set but not dried hard, cut off all the foil that isn't glued. Now put another blob of epoxy on top of the first, making sure it covers all the toothpick ends. Let this blob set a little. While it is still flexible, add another blob of epoxy on top of the first and wrap the entire tail unit around the duck's body stone. The piece of foil helps to prevent the epoxy from getting on your fingers while you are molding the tail around the duck's body. Hold the tail in position with a piece of masking tape until the epoxy glue is hard and dry.

Duck ready for painting.

5. Once you have attached the tail to
   the duck, the whole piece can be
   painted with a coat of gesso. Be sure
   to cover the piece of foil still on the
   tail.

5

ESPECIALLY FOR CHILDREN

Children can, of course, paint all manner of wonderful designs on single rocks, using their imaginations to create greeting "cards," animal friends, and fantasies of every description. But when they start to work on assembled creatures, I must give a word of warning. Epoxy glue is not for children under the age of ten, at least not without adult supervision. White glue is the safest adhesive for youngsters to use. This need not cramp their style in any way. White glue takes longer to set hard, but most children are used to this limitation from using this sort of glue at school.

Make sure you have plenty of old newspapers to protect their work surface. Give them a good supply of additional materials such as felt, yarn for hair, string for tails, and any old beads you might have. And don't forget the ever-useful pipe cleaner.

This might be a good time to help your children make up a small batch of bread dough as a substitute for beads. It is also a useful material for molding ears and noses. To make this dough take two slices of packaged bread, the sort that children love because it is soft and gooey. Cut off the crusts, break the bread into small pieces, and put into a glass bowl. Add one tablespoon of white glue and mix together. When it is thoroughly blended, let your children pick it up and work it with their hands until it is smooth. At first you will think you have the wrong proportions of bread to glue because it is very sticky and seemingly unmaneagable. After a while, however, it will form a compact dough which will mold very easily. This dough will keep well in a plastic bag in the refrigerator for about a week. After it has been shaped and allowed to dry, it can be painted with acrylic paints and varnished. I am sure your particular young rock crafters will find many uses for it.

To help your children get started, I am including a few specific projects. Once they have learned the basics of rock crafting, encourage them to use their own ideas for further creations. Most children are far more capable than we adults think they are, and there is nothing as effective as craft work for stretching the imagination and strengthening the motor skills—not to mention the boost in self-confidence that comes with the joy of achievement.

Paperweights— for Christmas or Anytime

Three paperweights: Clockwise from left: Christmas tree—paper cutout glued to white-painted rock with white glue; man with hat—felt cutouts on white rock; angel—foil Christmas decoration stuck on colored felt and glued to natural-color rock.

Paperweights

Materials
Flattish rocks or pebbles
White glue
Acrylic paints and felt-tipped pens
Acrylic polymer gloss medium
Scraps of felt or closely woven cloth *
Designs cut from paper or pictures cut from old greeting cards
Scissors

*If you don't have any felt scraps around the house, most craft stores and many dime stores sell inexpensive squares of felt in a wonderful range of colors. Don't use fabrics with a coarse weave. They tend to unravel, and it is very difficult to cut small shapes from them.

131

1. Draw an outline of your rock on white paper and set the paper aside. Then, paint your rock all over with one color on the side where you intend to have your design. If it's a pretty stone to begin with and you don't want to paint it, varnish it all over with acrylic polymer gloss medium to make it shine. The bottom can be left unpainted so long as none of it shows when the rock is lying flat. The background should be a light color so that your design cutouts show up well. You can use nice bright colors as long as the cutouts really show up. If you start with a dark stone, paint it white all over first. Then paint it with the color you want it to be. Your colors will be brighter when they are painted over white.

2. While the paint is drying, work out your design on paper. Draw the design inside the rock outline that you made before, to be sure it will fit. Now cut out your design pieces and lay them on top of the design drawn on paper, to make sure they go together to your satisfaction. If you have trouble transferring your design from paper to felt, you can glue felt to the back of your paper design, let it dry, and cut out both paper and felt together. The only trouble with this method is that the felt is stiff when the glue dries, so that you'll have trouble molding your design around any bumps on your rock. So be brave

132

and try to cut it out directly, even if
you don't get it exactly right. You'll
probably like the finished piece anyway.

One word of caution: Don't try to
cut any intricate design shapes, especially in felt or cloth. It may stretch
and tear and then your whole design
may fall apart. Keep it simple, with
shapes as big as possible. You'll find
them easier to handle.

3. By this time, your painted rock will
probably be dry enough to handle.
Place your design pieces on your
rock to make sure it still looks right.
Then carefully put a dab of white
glue on the back of each piece and
stick it on your rock. Glue one piece
at a time. Lay it face down on newspaper or some other scrap paper. Put
a spot of glue on the back and smear
it around with your finger to cover all
the surface, especially the edges.
Next—and this is important—wipe
wipe your fingers clean of all glue before you pick up your design, so that
you don't accidentally get glue on the
front side. Then carefully place each
piece in position and press it down,
especially around the edges to make
sure it's firmly in place.

You can add decorations beyond
the basic shape by gluing other small
cutout pieces on top of the first. If
you want to be really clever, you can
cut a group of pieces to fit together
like a jigsaw puzzle so that there are

no bumps showing. That may be difficult for small hands, however. The easier stick-on-top method is just as effective.

4. When the design is done, stick a piece of felt on the bottom of the stone. This will make a nice, soft, nonslip base that won't scratch polished surfaces.

Paperweights don't, of course, have to be flat stones, but they should have at least one more-or-less flat surface for a base. If you have a humpbacked stone, you can always make a repeat pattern around it by cutting the same design several times and sticking the pieces around your stone at regular intervals. Another possibility for circling a humpbacked stone is to cut a band of paper long enough to wrap all the way around your stone. Then fold the paper several times and cut out a string of paper dolls so that the design is joined at the ends of the arms. You have to make the design small enough to bend around the contours of your stone. In case you've forgotten, here's an illustration of how to cut out a string of paper dolls.

Band of paper marked into squares.

Folded band with outline of figure drawn on it.

String of paper dolls.

Mother's or Father's Day Rock Greetings

Try to make this greeting really personal. Take a pencil and paper into a corner somewhere and try to write a short message or poem telling your Mom or Dad how you feel about her or him. I'll bet you'll be surprised at the pleasure they'll get from your greeting.

135

Mother's Day Rock Greeting

Materials

A stone flat and smooth enough to
write a message on
White glue
Felt or paper cutouts for design
Scissors
Acrylic paint in white and whatever color
you want for your rock greeting
Acrylic polymer gloss medium
Felt-tipped pen, with a point fine enough
to enable you to write all of your mes-
sage.
Artist's fixative (if your pen does not
have waterproof ink)

1. Lay your rock on white paper and
   draw its outline so you can work out
   your design on paper before you start
   decorating the rock. This way you'll
   be sure to have enough room for
   both the design and the message.

136

2. Paint your rock all over with white
   acrylic paint or gesso. When it is dry,
   paint it with your chosen finish color.
   Make sure it is a light color that will
   allow your written message to show
   up.

3. While the paint is drying, work out
   your message. Try out different ways
   of placing the words and the design
   on your paper pattern. When you are
   satisfied with your arrangement on
   paper and the base coat of paint on
   your rock is dry, write your message
   on the rock with a felt-tipped pen in
   the space you have planned for it.
   Use a strong color—black, red, blue,
   or purple—because it will show up
   better. Leave it a few minutes to dry
   and then spray the whole rock with
   artist's fixative and let that dry, too.

   There's no easy way to transfer the
   lettering from paper to rock. Just
   be courageous and write it on directly. If you make a mistake, you
   can paint over it and start again.

4. Get your design pieces, lay them face
   down on paper, and apply glue to the
   back of each piece. Make sure that
   you cover the piece completely.
   Smear the glue with your fingers all
   over the back of the piece, right to
   the edges. Remember—before you
   do anything else, you have to clean
   the glue off your fingers. Now you
   can apply your design pieces, one at
   a time, to your rock.

   There are two reasons why it is

better to put the design on after the message. First, it lets you spray fixative on the writing without messing up your design pieces. Secondly, if your message turns out to take up more or less space on your stone than it did on paper, you can always make your design smaller or larger as necessary. If you want to embellish your greeting even further, you can add tiny flowers drawn on with felt-tipped pens. Do this along with your message so that when you spray with fixative, your lettering and your decorations will both be fixed.

A Furry Hedgehog
(See also Color Plate 10)

Furry Hedgehog

While the average hedgehog (for instance, the porcupine) is distinctly unpleasant to pick up and cuddle because of his sharp quills, this furry rock creature is quite the reverse. He is fun to fondle and stroke and really very easy to make.

Almost any roundish rock will do if you'd like to make one like him. It's best to have a stone which is rounded on top, so that it looks like an animal curled up. Here's how you go about making this lovable creature.

Materials

A roundish rock

A piece of fur fabric (Do you have an old
fur fabric garment that is of no more
use?)

Three small pebbles for eyes and nose
(Small beads or bread dough can also be
used for eyes and nose.)

White glue

Masking tape

A black felt-tipped pen

Acrylic paint in the color you want, if
your stone's natural color isn't right

Acrylic polymer gloss medium, so your
hedgehog will have a nice smooth face

1. Decide which end of your rock is
   going to be the face. Then mark with
   pencil the spots where you want the
   eyes and nose. Keep all three marks
   close together, leaving room under
   the nose for a mouth. Hedgehogs
   have very small, smooth-skinned
   faces. The quills (in your hedgehog's
   case fur) start quite close to the top
   of the eyes.

2. Have three pieces of masking tape
   handy to hold each eye and the nose
   in position after you have attached
   them to the head with a spot of white
   glue. Glue and tape each feature one
   at a time, so it doesn't slide out of
   position while you are doing the next.
   Leave the hedgehog overnight, or at
   least a few hours, so the glue can set
   before you attempt to put his fur coat
   on. When the glue is dry (when it

139

looks clear instead of white) carefully remove the tape.

3. Now you can paint his face any color you want, if you don't like his natural color. Paint far enough back down the body so that the edge of the paint will be covered when you put the fur fabric on. Don't worry if paint gets on the eyes and nose. You will paint them over anyway.

4. When the face is dry, use a color that will stand out against the face color to paint the eyes and nose. Now add a mouth. If you want the hedgehog to have a startled expression, paint in eyebrows. When the facial features are dry, finish the painted part of the rock with a gloss varnish or polymer gloss medium.

5. Get your piece of fur fabric and measure your hedgehog for his fur coat. Measure the distance around his fattest part and add a half inch to overlap; then measure the rock from where the hairline will be to the end of the tail and add a half inch for this dimension. Use a piece of string to measure with if you don't have a tape measure.

After you have measured your hedgehog, cut a rectangular piece of fur fabric in the correct size. You will find that there is a direction to most fur fabrics. That is, the hairs naturally lie flatter in one direction than in the other. If your fabric is like this, cut

your fur so that the hairs lie back
from your hedgehog's face rather
than forward over his eyebrows like
bangs. Remember that you want the
fur to look like quills sticking up. It is
best to cut fur fabric from the back
side of the fabric using a razor blade
so that you don't cut the hairs as
much and therefore it's less messy.
But get your mother, father, or some
adult to do this for you, because razor
blades can be very dangerous. If you
cut it yourself, you can use scissors,
but cut it on a large piece of newspaper so you can catch all the loose
hair that will come off. Shake the fabric over the paper to make sure all
the hairs are gone.

6. Wrap the fur around the hedgehog's
body to make sure it's big enough.
It's better to have it a bit on the big
side at this stage rather than too
small. Make sure the hairs are lying in
the right direction. Put a thick line of
white glue down the center of the
fabric (nose end to tail end) and
spread it with your fingers to about
one third of the fabric's width. Clean
your fingers and lay the fabric on the
hedgehog's back, just a bit back from
the eyes. Cover the paint line if you
painted his face. Press the fabric
down and then let it sit for a bit while
you think about the next step.

7. Lay the hedgehog on his back on
newspaper. Make five or six cuts
through the fur fabric, starting from

the outside edges and cutting up to
where the back is glued. Pull the
pieces over him in pairs from each
side and from the rear. Trim off any
excess except for a small overlap on
all pieces. This means you will be cutting off small pieces shaped like pie
slices. Shake out all the loose hairs
that will result from the cutting and
put him back down on his back, belly
up, on a piece of newspaper.

8. Now put glue on all the wrong side of
the fabric that is showing, using a
finger to make sure you get the glue
to the fabric edges. Now wash your
fingers, but don't take all day about
it, because you don't want your glue
to dry while you are gone. With your
clean fingers, pull each glued section
up and around his tummy, starting
with the two pieces nearest his face,
then the two pieces on the other end,
and lastly those in between. You will
have to overlap them a bit to go
around the curve of your rock and
stretch them at the same time. When
all the pieces are down in position,
squeeze him gently all round with
your hands to make sure all the
edges are down tight. When the glue
is dry, ruffle his fur so the seams
don't show and he's ready to be
loved.

Dotted lines showing
cuts in fur fabric.

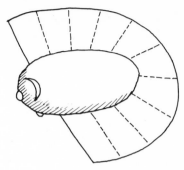

Cut strips with overlaps
removed.

First strip glued around
body.

Gluing partially com-
pleted.

Long-Haired Clown

This friendly little fellow is made from a single humpbacked stone. Here is how you can make one like him.

Long-Haired Clown

Materials

Roundish, hump-backed stone for the head
Small round bead for a nose
Scraps of felt for ears, eyes, mouth, and tongue
Yarn for hair
Acrylic paint
and white glue.

1. Paint the stone white. Add a dab of pink where you want the cheeks to be. Next put a dab of white glue where you want the nose to be, and sit the bead that will become his nose in position on the white glue. Either use masking tape to hold the nose in position, or prop the stone somewhere so the nose bead stays in place without sliding off or out of position. Since white glue takes rather a long

time to dry, leave the rock overnight or for several hours at least, before proceeding with the next steps.

2. Once your clown's nose is fixed in position, you can work on the rest of his face. Cut out two circles of blue felt (or brown, if you like brown eyes best) and two smaller circles of black felt for pupils. Glue the larger circles in position on either side of and slightly above the nose. Then glue the smaller black circles on top of the larger, colored ones. If you don't stick the small black circles exactly in the middle of the larger ones, you can make your clown look left, right, or even make him cross his eyes. Just experiment a bit before you glue them in position, to see which looks best to you.

   If you would like a popeyed clown, use a couple of small beads or pebbles as eyeballs either glued directly to your rock like the nose, or glued on top of the larger circles of felt instead of the small black felt circles.

3. Cut a red felt mouth of whatever size and shape pleases you most. Make sure it will fit under your clown's nose and then glue it in position. If you want a tongue sticking out, as ours has, cut an open mouth from your red felt (just cut a small hole in the middle of the felt mouth). Then cut out a red felt tongue-shaped piece. Glue the end of the tongue-shaped piece on front and back for about an

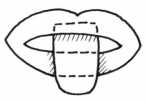

eighth of an inch and tuck it up under the clown's top lip.

4. Cut the ears from pink felt. Cut four pieces about the shape of a somewhat flattened keyhole and glue them together in pairs, leaving the straight-edged part unglued for later attachment to the head. When they are dry enough not to come apart, glue the inside of the straight-edged parts of both ears and stick them to your clown's head, one on either side, about in line with his eyes and nose.

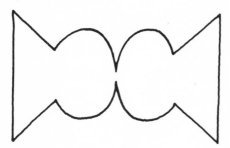

Felt for ears.

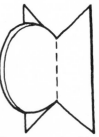

Ear pieces glued together.

Don't worry about the part where they attach to his head, because that will be covered up with hair when you give him some.

5. Hair is the last step. You can cut this while the ears dry. Cut your yarn into pieces. The length depends upon the size of your clown and the length of hair you want him to have. Cut it longer than you think you'll need, because you can always give him a haircut after the hair is stuck on. Just how

146

much hair you give him and whether you leave a bald spot is up to you.

If you use thick wool, it's better to unravel the ends a bit before you glue it on. Then, when the glue is dry, unravel the rest of the wool so each strand gives you lots of thinner strands.

Don't worry if you can't get enough strands on with the first layer to make his hair as thick as you would like. You can always make him hairier by adding a second and third layer of yarn on top of the first. When your clown is hairy enough to suit your taste and the glue is dry, you can rearrange the strands and trim them to your satisfaction—long or short, bangs or no bangs, eyes showing or not.

If you'd like your clown to have a beanie hat, cut a circle of felt and glue it over the place where your strands of yarn hair come together. Glue a piece of felt on the base of your creation to protect whatever your clown rests on, and he is complete.

Spotted Spiny Alligator

(See also Color Plate 11)

This long bumpy creature, which I painted white with orange spots and green spikes, is fun to have around. Here's what you'll need to make one just like him.

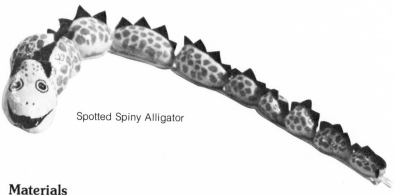

Spotted Spiny Alligator

Materials

A bunch of pebbles of gradually decreasing size (This one used eleven. The biggest was about an inch long and the smallest about half an inch long. All were somewhat smaller in width than length.) A strip of tape or braid about the width of your smallest pebble and just a bit longer than all your pebbles laid end to end

Some bright-colored felt to make the
spikes—your choice of color
White glue
Acrylic paint to make the spots
Gesso to base coat all the pebbles first
A fine black felt-tipped pen to draw the
face

1. Paint all your stones with gesso or
   white acrylic. Then paint them again
   with whatever background color you
   want your alligator to be. Lay them
   on old newspaper to do the painting.
   Paint everything you can reach with
   the brush, leaving just the part that's
   actually touching the newspaper unpainted. Select one pebble for the
   head and paint a face on it. I was
   lucky enough to find a pebble that
   sloped down at one end with bumps
   in the right places to make a forehead
   and nose. But a face on any stone
   will look fine when you've made it
   up. When the face you've made with
   felt-tipped pens is dry, spray the head
   with artist's fixative. Or coat it with
   acrylic polymer gloss medium, if you
   used acrylic paints. While not essential, the fixative or finish will protect
   colors and features from dirt and possible smudging.
2. Lay out your pebbles in a straight line,
   starting with the head stone, then in
   descending order of size down to the
   tail. You'll probably have to play with
   them a bit to find which way they
   look best. Have a slight space be-

tween each pebble, about as wide as the thickness of a paper match from a matchbook. Measure the length of your line of pebbles and cut your braid or tape that length. Glue the bottom or unpainted part of each pebble to the tape with white glue. Set it on the tape in the same order you had them originally, starting with the head and leaving the same paper match distance between each. Leave your alligator to dry in position. This will take several hours. With care you can proceed to the next step before the glue holding the pebbles to the tape is completely hard—provided that you don't move the alligator while you work.

3. The next step is to put his spiky spine on. This is made from a lot of small triangles of felt. The same triangular shapes will make ears also. The spike triangles must get smaller toward the tail, where the pebbles are smaller, so that they look in the right proportion.

    Cut a strip of felt about six inches long and three eighths of an inch wide at one end, running down to about three sixteenths of an inch wide at the other. Felt squares from the store usually come in pieces that are about nine inches by twelve, so you can just cut your strip off one of the short sides. Naturally, if your stones are bigger or smaller than those I used, or if you want bigger or smaller spikes down your alligator's

Felt strip for spikes.

back, you can make your strip wider
or narrower to suit. The important
thing is to cut it wider at one end than
at the other so that you end up with a
bunch of triangles that get smaller and
smaller. Now with scissors cut your
strip along the dotted lines as shown.
You'll get a nice lot of triangular
pieces. Leave them in a line as you
cut them so that you can use them in
the same order as you glue them on
your alligator's back.

These tiny pieces of felt will be very
difficult to handle if you try to glue
them along one edge, so the best
way is to put the glue along the alligator's back. Do this one pebble at a
time, running a small bead of glue
across the center of each pebble from
front to back, starting with the first
pebble behind the head stone.

Now pick up your triangular pieces
of felt one at a time and stand them
upright on the line of glue (a pair of
tweezers may come in handy). Stick
the longest edge of each triangle to
the glue line. You may have to press
the points of each triangle down to
make it follow the curve of the
pebble. You can do this easily with
the point of a pencil or your tweezers,
while you hold the felt by the top of
the triangle. Do the same thing with
each pebble right down to the tail.

4. Attach the ears to the head stone the
   same way. Two medium-sized triangles of felt, like the spike triangles

from the middle of the strip, will work well. Put them on at an angle, with the front point being about in line with the outside of the eyes and the two black points coming slightly together toward the back of the head.

5. Paint the body. The spots should be irregularly shaped, with white spaces between. The spots should get smaller down toward the tail as the pebbles and spikes get smaller—keep everything in proportion. The spots on the head are bigger at the back and get smaller fast as you paint down toward the facial features.

6. Carefully paint the pebbles from spiky spine down to the tape with acrylic polymer gloss medium.

All this should be done without moving the pebbles from the original straight-line position in which you glued them on the tape. Leave the whole creation on newspaper to dry until morning. At this point, trim off any excess tape at the tail.

One word of caution about this alligator. If you want to pick him up and move him around much after he's made, don't use pebbles much more than an inch in diameter or they will be too heavy for the glue and tape to support.

GROUPINGS, SETTINGS, AND UTILITARIAN USES

Once you have created a number of different people and animals, you will find that they can be arranged together to make interesting scenes such as are shown in some of the color plates in this book. To do this, your figures or animals have to be more or less in proportion to each other and to any ancillary elements you introduce into the scene.

You can, of course, start out with a group scene in mind—like the two conversing farmers described in chapter 3—and build your scene from scratch. But you'll find it surprising how easily your creations seem to go together to make groups, even though you didn't have that in mind to begin with. Perhaps because they are all made of rocks, they have a natural affinity for other rock creatures.

Pairs of human figures have a lot of potential, and pairs

153

of animals likewise. A large and small two-figure combination will inevitably end up looking like parent and child unless you paint them otherwise. They could of course also be made to represent David and Goliath, teacher and student, or circus strong man and midget. It all depends upon your point of view.

Don't overlook the possibility of introducing non-pebble elements to add background to a group setting. Try your rock creatures and pebble people in conjunction with a plant grouping. These critters can look cute peeking through the petals. A large cake-tin lid sprinkled with sand or sawdust could easily become a circus ring for some clown figures or the circus rider described in chapter 4.

If you live near a source of flat pebbles—a beach is probably the best bet, or the bed of a shallow, fast-running stream—then you have the ideal makings for bas-relief pebble pictures. If you're going to make one, spend some time putting your pebbles together into many different arrangements of people and groupings before you go to your epoxy glue, because you'll find that any group of pebbles can be assembled in many, many different ways to make many different pictures. And you might find a much happier grouping if you try a number of different arrangements before "freezing the mold."

Such pebble pictures can be made on almost any background, as long as it contrasts sufficiently with your stones. You don't want them to disappear into a busy background pattern. So keep it plain or at least contrasting in some way with your pebbles. Naturally, if you use a soft cloth background, you'll have to glue the cloth to plywood or some such rigid material before you can hang your picture on the wall.

If you enjoy flower arranging, try your rock craft there, too. An arrangement with a pebble person or creature can look delightfully different. The Japanese do wonderful things with rocks and pebbles in their flower arrangements, using natural stones just as they are found. So if you come across some beautiful pebbles that seem just too nice on their own to incorporate into any figure, just wash and varnish them and keep them for your next Oriental flower arrangement. Of course, such natural beauties can also look attractive just varnished and sitting alone on a shelf.

UTILITARIAN ROCK CREATIONS

Two useful ways in which to incorporate rocks into your home decor are as doorstops and bookends. Any big handsome rock, washed and varnished, will serve either of these purposes all on its own if it has one relatively flat side to sit on. Or you might want to be more creative and turn your doorstop into a doorman like the following figure.

Pierre the Doorman

This was a fat, heavy rock about six inches high, nicely rounded and quite smooth when found. He sat in my garden all one summer, after working his way to the surface in the spring, as rocks seem sometimes to do. While I waited for some inspiration to hit, Pierre (as he later became) got washed clean by summer rain and spent a spell as a gate stop.

When I decided to bring him into the house and turn him into a door stop, I added head and arms. If you make one, it's best done in position against any door. First, lay a piece of aluminum foil on the floor and up the door past where the top of your rock will be. Then attach his head stone with epoxy glue, simply resting the head stone on the body stone and leaning it against the door until set. His arms, upraised in an attitude of Gallic surprise, are glued and taped in position until they dry, leaning backwards slightly so they touch the door also.

Now give your doorman a coat of gesso, followed by any decorative painting you have in mind. Whether you give your doorman foot stones or not depends upon how flat your basic body stone is. Ours didn't need feet to stand upright and they aren't really missed.

Bookends

Holding up books is another simple and effective use for rocks and pebbles. Their natural weight makes them very practical, although they may take up more space than the conventional kind. To make a pair, all you need is a pile of rocks joined together with epoxy glue. Here's how to go about it.

1. Wrap a book in aluminum foil to protect it. Stand it on end on another sheet of aluminum foil.
2. Place the two biggest rocks from your collection, one on either side of your foil-wrapped book, and touching it.

With epoxy, glue other rocks and pebbles to the first one on each side of your foil-wrapped book, until you create a roughly triangular shape on either side. Build up the thickness of these triangular shapes on each side of the book, keeping the stones against the book on one side of each triangle and against the foil base on the other. How big you make your rock piles depends upon how big and heavy you want your bookends. And that depends on the size of the books that they are designed to support.

Be sparing with your epoxy. You don't want it to run down and show on the outside of your bookends. For any pebbles in the middle of each pile, of course, that's not a consideration. How many pebbles you use also depends upon how big your pebbles are and how big you want your bookends to be. You might make a pair with just two or three stones on each side, or you might use dozens.

3. If you have a collection of varied and attractive colored stones, you may decide that they look best in their natural colors and textures. In that case, just make sure they are clean and finish them either with polymer gloss medium or any varnish you have on hand. If their natural colors are not very interesting, you can have fun painting all or some of your rock

157

piles. Consider painting floral designs on some in bright colors, or putting faces on a few peeking out from your rocky bookends. When you're all done painting and varnishing, you might find it necessary to add feet to your bookends. But try them out first.

4. If the bookends tend to slide apart from the weight of books between them, the addition of feet that go under the first book or two will usually cure the problem. These feet are attached to the base of each rock pile, extending a few inches so that the first few books will sit on them and so prevent the bookends from slipping.

5. You can make a foot for each bookend from a piece of thin copper sheet (easily obtainable at art and craft supply stores), some other flat metal, or even a piece of cardboard. Just glue it to the base of each rock pile, extending about three inches from the vertical side. If you use metal, attach the foot with epoxy glue. If you use cardboard, white glue will be fine. Also, if you use metal, make sure that the edges are smooth enough not to scratch your shelves. Cut the corners round instead of square and smooth all edges with a fine file or emery cloth.

Bookend foot.

ANCILLARY ITEMS

With various projects in this book, non-pebble ancilliary items have been shown and described—such as the accountant's calculator, the witch's broom, the cave-man's spear. All quite simply made and designed to add a touch of realism to the project. Here we will describe a few other things you can make without too much trouble or any special tools. Doubtless you will think of many others to make yourself.

Lamp Post

In one of the color plates, an old-fashioned lamp post is shown. It was made in an hour or so from workshop scraps. If your scene would be enhanced by a lamp post, here's how to make one just like it. The dimensions given produce a lamp post about six inches high. Of course, you may change size, materials or design to suit your particular application.

1. Start with a piece of dowel rod 5'' long and 3/16'' in diameter. This makes the main post. For the cross bar, cut two pieces of dowel rod 1'' long and ⅛'' diameter.

If you don't have dowel rod, it's not too difficult to round off any piece of soft wood for both upright and cross bar. In fact you could probably make both out

159

of aluminum wire, using epoxy glue to hold them together—then you could put a bend or two in the post if you wanted.

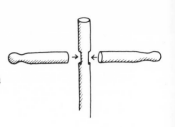

2. Assuming you are using wood, the next step is to shape the end of each 1″ piece for the cross bars to look like this.

3. Next, flatten off a small section (about ⅛″) on either side of the main post, about ½″ from the top. Alternatively, dig out a slight depression there in which to glue the ends of each cross bar. This will hold better than a butt joint. Glue the two cross bars into position with white glue and use masking tape to hold them in position till they dry.

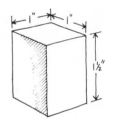

4. While they are drying, you can make the lamp post head from either a block of balsa wood or, as I used, a block of Styrofoam. You'll need a squared off block of either balsa or Styrofoam about 1½″ long by 1″ square like this. If you don't have a block, make one by glueing two or three pieces of balsa together with the grain running the long way of the block, as shown. Use white glue and leave the block to dry overnight, either in a vise, or under some weight.

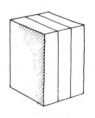

5. When your block is ready, draw a line around it, ½″ from one end (which will become the top of your lamp) to mark the fattest part.

6. From the ends of this line, on two opposite sides of your block, draw

lines that come together at the top
of your block, and slope in toward
each other on the longer (bottom)
end to points $5/16''$ from each side,
leaving a $3/8''$ gap between them.

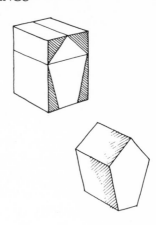

7. Now cut away all the material outside those lines (the shaded area
shown) until you end up with a
shape like this.

8. Repeat the sloping lines on the
other two sides (this will be the sides
you have just cut) and cut off top
and bottom of those two sides also,
until you have a shape like this.

9. Now bore a hole $^3/_{16}''$ in diameter in the bottom of your lamp head to take the post. If you don't have a drill, a good enough hole can be poked with the point of a scissor or knife if you are careful. Try the post to make sure it fits, then fix it permanently with white glue.

10. Whether you put a base on your lamp or not depends on whether you want it movable or permanently attached to some scene. If permanent, the next step is to glue it in position with epoxy glue, tape it and wait for the glue to set before painting it. If you want a movable lamp, you'll need to make a base for it to stand on. Use anything flat, and a little heavier than your total lamp post. A piece of ¼-inch plywood about one inch across should do, but you could also use a discarded paint jar lid. Another base, equally steady, could be made from a cone of thin cardboard glued around the base. Or if you have some play dough, bread dough, or papier mâché handy, you could form a base with any one of them, perhaps shaping it to look like a rock-pile from which the lamp post is emerging.

11. The last step is to paint your lamp post to fit the scene you have it planned for. If you used a Styrofoam head, you'll only need to paint the top and edges black. The white

of the Styrofoam will look like glass panels where you don't paint it. If you made the head of wood, you'll need to paint it white first, then add the black lines and top. You may also decide that your "glass" panels look best painted yellow to resemble an old-fashioned gas lamp. We painted our lamp post green, but of course you'll paint yours to suit your own taste.

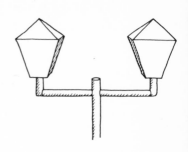

It's easy to make a variation on this lamp post, with a different shape for the top, or a multiple head. You might make a modern-looking lamp standard using four small Styrofoam balls on a cross, using the same basic construction techniques just described.

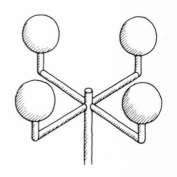

Bench

A simple bench on which you might construct a seated pebble person can be made very easily from three flat pieces of balsa wood glued together. You can also use two sections of twig (with the bark left on) for the legs, to make a rustic-looking bench.

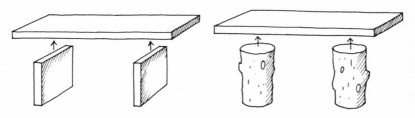

163

Hydrant

A fire hydrant is easy to make from three
pieces of dowel rod whittled with a knife
or shaped with a file, glued together, and
painted red.

Many different accessories can be
made from simple rectangular blocks of
balsa wood, sometimes with no additional shaping, but painted to resemble
everyday articles such as TV set, cam-
eras, cabinets, desks, etc. And things like
walking sticks, cigars and pipes, crutches,
canes, and so on are easily made from
small pieces of balsa, with a little imagination.

Thin copper wire is a useful accessory
builder to have around. It was used for
several objects accompanying projects in
this book and you'll no doubt find other
uses for it.

Wire and Rock Tree

This wintry-looking, gnarled, wind-bent tree is made of copper wire, one rough-shaped rock, and epoxy glue to hold wire to rock. There is also a piece of felt on the base to avoid possible scratches from the ends of the wire. It is charming all alone, or as a background for pebble people or creatures. The size of tree you make has some bearing on the thickness and amount of wire you'll need, so I'll give the steps for the one shown here, which is about 6½ inches high, including its rock base.

1. Cut off a 4-foot piece of 24-gauge copper wire. Fold this in half, and then in half again, so that you have a folded four-strand piece that's twelve inches long. Don't worry if you're not exact—you'll just end up with a slightly longer or shorter branch.

   Now you need a pair of snub-nosed pliers and a vise, or two pairs of pliers and a helper to hold one pair of pliers for you. Grip the end of your four-strand wire where there is one fold and two cut ends, in the vise—or have your helper hold them in the second pair of pliers. About ¼'' to ½'' of the end should be gripped in the jaws of vise or pliers.

   Now grip the other end of your four-strand wire (the end with two loops) with your own pliers, with about ¾'' held in the plier jaws. With the vise or helper end held still, pull gently to keep the wires taut and straight, while twisting the pliers in your hands as shown (A). You'll find it probably needs both hands to do this without the wires springing loose out from the end of your pliers. Keep twisting in one direction until you have a single strand that's twisted neatly from end to end, all except the two loops you've been twisting from. It should now look like the illustration (B). Now either twist up, or cut off the ends held in the vise or your helper's pliers so it's twisted right to the end at that end of the strand.

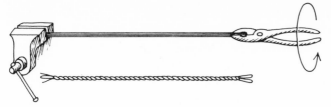

Repeat this process until you have 20 to 24 four-wire twisted strands. Because you'll want some strands longer and some shorter to make branches of various lengths, start out with some 36-inch lengths of wire, some 44-inch, some 40-inch, some 54-inch. The precise length isn't really important. You just need to end up with a variety of lengths of four-strand twisted pieces.

2. When all your four-strand pieces are done, take them in two's and three's and twist them together to make fatter strands. You can do this with your fingers alone. Twist them together from the cut end, holding the cut end of two strands between thumb and forefinger of one hand while twisting them together with thumb and fore-finger of the other. Let the strands merge together naturally. The curves of one strand will fit into the curves of the other. Leave these multiple strands untwisted for about an inch and a half at the loop ends of the wires. This will make the ends of the branches where they separate and get thinner. Having no cut ends will make it easier on your fingers later on.

3. Continue combining the twisted
   strands till you have four or five fat
   ones, which will become both main
   roots and main branches. Now start
   combining these fat branches into
   one trunk about three inches from
   what will be the "root" ends (that's
   the ends where the cut pieces of wire
   are) and twist them together to form
   the main trunk for about three inches
   more. At this point, you take the two
   longest of your fat branches, and
   twist those two together for another
   inch or so.
4. Find a suitable rock for your base. Arrange the root ends to wrap around
   it, conforming to any bumps that are
   there. A bumpy rock looks best for a
   tree base, so don't waste your
   smooth ones here.
5. Make the roots bend and twist
   around the rock till you're happy with
   their position and then fix them there
   with epoxy glue using tape or a vice
   to hold them in position. The roots
   should be long enough, or the stone
   small enough, for the roots to disappear under the lower curve of your
   rock. Unravel and flatten that part of
   each root which is under your rock so
   it lies as flat as possible. Then when
   the epoxy is dry, add a piece of felt to
   cover the bottom of your stone and
   the ends of the wire.
6. Now that the bottom is fixed, you can
   turn your attention to the tree proper.
   If you want a storm-bent look, you

need to end up with most of the
branch ends pointing in the same direction. For a tree clinging to a rock,
this seems to look best. However,
there's nothing to stop you having
your tree any shape that pleases you.
7. Bend the main trunk into the shape
   you want. Work out progressively to
   thinner and thinner branches, bend-
   ing and shaping as you go. At this
   stage, you'll probably want to unwind
   some of the twisted together strands a
   bit at various places to get the random look of our tree. This is fine,
   because you'll find it gets to look
   even more gnarled that way.

You may want to cut some of the
branches shorter to fit your design. But
try to keep the cutting for last, or you
may find the spiky ends of the cut wire
puncturing your fingers as you work on
other branches. To cut the twisted wires,
you'll need a pair of wire cutters. Household scissors will easily cut a single strand
of 24-gauge copper wire without damag-
ing the scissors, but anything thicker than
that may harm them. So if you want to
cut a thicker strand either use wire-cut-
ters or unravel your strand till you can
cut it one strand at a time—and cut as
far back from the tips of your scissors as
possible.
8. After the tree is all shaped, untwist
   the four-strand loops a bit making
   them into two-strand branch ends.
   Then cut open all the loops and sepa-

rate the single strands to become our tree twigs.

Copper wire is soft and easy to bend and is thus more suitable than brass or steel. Silver is fine, if you're affluent and know a jeweler's supply house to get it from.

Note: Your copper wire will shine beautifully when new, but copper tarnishes after a while. If that bothers you, lacquer it with clear nail varnish or commercial acetate varnish. You'll find the best stage to do this is after making the initial four-strand lengths. Dip one end in the varnish and stroke the brush up until it's covered, then hang each strand by a dressmaker's pin from a shelf edge to dry. It's almost impossible to varnish a finished tree—apart from the difficulty of getting at it all, and getting spiked as you do, you lose track of what's varnished and what isn't.

APPENDIX:
A GUIDE TO
PRODUCTS
USED FOR
ROCK CRAFTING

The products listed in this appendix are all useful for rock crafting—and other crafts as well. Some have many applications; others have minor uses. We trust the list will be helpful to you in selecting products and materials.

ADHESIVES

White glue is the generic name for such brands as Elmer's and Sobo, most of which come in both plastic squeeze bottles with pointed dispenser tips and large, bulk-quantity jars.

White glue has a wide number of uses and is the sort recommended for use by children in this book. Its advantages are:

- It is the strongest adhesive for porous materials such as paper, cardboard, fabric.

- It is one of the most permanent adhesives.

- It can be diluted with water and applied with a soft brush when a thin coating is needed, though this is not an application used with pebble craft.

- It is appropriate for all ages from elementary school on up, and even younger with supervision.

It has some minor disadvantages:

- Once it dries, it cannot be washed out of clothing or other fabrics.

- It causes colored tissue and crepe paper to bleed and wrinkle. (If a test sample of paper you want to use for découpage to a rock bleeds or wrinkles, use contact cement instead.)

To apply white glue, always smooth the squeezed-out ribbon of glue with the fingertips (moistened if necessary). To speed adhesion, let the glue become slightly tacky before pressing the surfaces together. Some white glue is manufactured with formulas that make them quicker setting or tackier. The trade names they are sold under are usually variations descriptive of these qualities.

Specialized Adhesives
For more difficult attachment problems there are specialized adhesives formulated for different purposes. Read the labels carefully before you buy them, to make sure they are suitable for the purpose you have in mind. Many of them warn against use by children.

APPENDIX

Epoxy adhesive is usually a two-part compound (a glue and a hardener) which is mixed just prior to use. It forms a strong and permanent bond between non-porous surfaces and is the most suitable adhesive to use in joining rocks together. It is, in fact, stronger than most rocks. If you drop a pebble person, the break will usually occur in the pebble rather than the epoxy glue that is used. It is for this reason that we recommend spreading the glue over the surface of each pebble beyond the actual area of contact in any join. Epoxy is, however, very toxic, and should only be used by adults or with supervision, mature children.

Contact cement forms an instant bond without holding or clamping, but only after the cement has been partly dried on each surface to be joined for 15 or more minutes. It is used primarily where one or both surfaces to be joined consist of a non-porous material such as metal or plastic, but it needs a larger area of surface contact than epoxy. This is the glue used for attaching veneers to wood surfaces. It may also be used for attaching paper, where it is necessary to avoid the wrinkling which white glue sometimes causes on thin paper. Because of label cautions, it should be used only by adults or, with supervision, mature children.

At least two companies (Weldwood and Elmer's) have introduced a contact cement that is water-based and non-toxic—and which could therefore safely be used by younger children. However, because it is water-based, it has the same wrinkling characteristics as white glue on thin paper.

Several *acrylic mediums* are occasionally used as adhesives. They are described with all the other acrylic products in the section on paints that follows.

Caution
Beware of the instant-bonding adhesives on the market which contain cyanoacrylate. This is the adhesive which advertises that "one drop will hold a ton," or some similar claim. The claim is factually correct. It is that strong and that fast. It is very easy to accidentally bond two fingers or finger

173

and thumb together with this glue so that surgery is necessary to part them. It is risky stuff to keep in a household where there are children and it is for this reason that in this book we do not recommend its use.

PAINTS AND VARNISHES

Acrylic paints are more useful for more purposes than any other paints, which is why we recommend them over such standbys as tempera (liquid or powder) or oils. Technically known as "acrylic polymer latex emulsion" paints, acrylics are water-thinnable when wet, but permanently waterproof when dry. However, the dried paints are easily stripped from hands and non-porous surfaces (formica, plastics, metal) under warm water. Once dry, they are impossible to remove from fabric and from paint brushes, so remember to wash brushes as soon as you're done with them and wash out of clothes immediately should you get it on them. Be sure, also, to caution children about these points before you turn them loose with paints and brushes.

Acrylic paints come in two forms:

Jar paints, usually sold in hobby and craft stores, have the consistency of sour cream and dry to an opaque matte finish. They are the best for most craft projects but may be more than you need for pebble painting, unless you're going into it wholesale, or will be using these paints for other craft projects.

Tube paints, usually sold in art supply stores, have a toothpaste-like consistency and dry to a semi-gloss finish. For most crafts projects, they should be thinned with either acrylic matte medium to reduce gloss or gloss medium to enhance it, depending on what you want. Water may also be used as a thinner, but not more than the amount of medium added, otherwise the binding quality of the paint will be reduced too much. For some pebble projects, you'll find it easier to just dip the point of a brush into the tube rather than squeezing paint out, because the quantities you'll need are so small.

If you're going out to buy acrylic paints for your pebble craft, avoid the jars that come in prepacked set of six jars; they are generally of poor quality and too thin to give good coverage. Small tubes of the colors you want are probably the best starting place.

Mediums contain the same polymer binders as the pigments; they are used to thin paints without reducing their adhesive qualities. There are two kinds of medium:

- *Gloss medium* adds a high luster to the pigment. In addition to thinning, it has two other uses as a varnish over acrylic paints when a high luster is required and as a glue if you are sticking several layers of thin paper on a stone to build up a design.

- *Matte medium* reduces the luster of the pigment. In some brands matte medium is also used as a varnish; in other brands matte medium and matte varnish are two separate products.

Acrylic gesso is a white painting base which can be used as a primer on any surface, even plastic or metal, and can be covered with any kind of paint. It is a most useful undercoating when you want to conceal the color of the original item or when you want to smooth out a slightly rough surface as some stones have.

Acrylic gel is an extra-thick gloss medium which can be used as an adhesive that will partially embed three-dimensional objects such as seeds, beans, beads, or buttons used as decorative features on your rocks.

Acrylic modelling paste is a mortar-like substance which can also be used for embedding three-dimensional objects on the surface of your rocks.

Felt-tip markers (wide tips) and *fiber-tip pens* (fine points) come in two forms: (1) with washable ink—that is, ink

that can be removed by washing; and (2) permanent, waterproof ink. Consider this when you give them to children to
use. Consider also that while the permanent ink pens and
markers can be varnished over, the water-soluble kind will
run unless you treat the drawing with artist's fixative before
varnishing. However, felt-tip pens and markers are useful
where it is necessary to have firm control over the color in a
small area.

Model airplane paints are glossy enamels suitable for
adults and children over the age of eight. They have two
main advantages. They come in tiny jars at a very low price,
so that a full range of colors can be purchased quite inexpen-
sively. The metallic gold, silver and copper colors in them are
very beautiful and useful. Their main disadvantage is that
cleanup after using them requires the use of turpentine or
paint thinner, which are best restricted to teenagers or older.
They are not recommended for any of the projects in this
book, but you might want to experiment with them because
of the metallic colors.

Oil paints are not recommended in this book because
they take a long time to dry and need turpentine or kerosene
for cleanups. Acrylic paints can do everything that oils can in
rock-painting easier and faster with less mess and easier
clean-up.

Artist's Fixative comes in an aerosol can and is meant for
sealing pencil, charcoal, and pastel drawings to stop smearing
or smudging. For our purposes in rock-painting, they also
seal water-soluble felt-tip pens and marker drawings so that
they can be worked on with acrylics or varnished with acrylic
varnish or polymer medium.

Acrylic varnishes are preferred whenever possible because they are non-toxic and can be used by comparatively
young children with safety. They *must* be used over:

• Permanent felt or fiber-tip markers and pens. (Any other
finish will cause those permanent inks to bleed.)

They *must not* be used over:

- Water-soluble paints, such as washable felt-tip markers and pens or tempera paints. (It makes these paints run unless they are first sprayed with artists fixative.)

They *may* be used over all other paints. Acrylic varnishes are available in both glossy and matte finishes.

Shellac and *varnish* are to some extent interchangeable. We don't recommend their use in this book, because acrylics, with their water solubility, are so much simpler to handle. However, since you may want to experiment with others, the chart below may be useful to you. The main differences between the two are:

- Shellac is cheaper and faster-drying.

- Varnish is more durable and slower drying.

	Shellac	*Varnish* *
Drying time for one coat	30 minutes	3 hours
Drying time for recoating	2–3 hours	Overnight
Solvent, thinner, and brush cleaner	Denatured alcohol	Turpentine or paint thinner or mineral spirits
Resistant to water	No	Yes
Resistant to alcohol	No	Yes
Suitable for outdoor use	No	Yes
Can be used as sealer *under*	All paints except felt-tip markers and fiber-tip pens	All paints except *permanent* felt-tip markers and fiber-tip pens
Can be used as finish *over*	All paints except *permanent* felt-tip markers and fiber-tip pens	All paints except *permanent* felt-tip markers and fiber-tip pens
Age range	Teens and adults	Teens and adults
Color	Almost clear	Amber cast
Consistency	Thin	Heavy

*There are several kinds of varnish on the market. The synthetics known as "polyurethane varnishes" are extremely strong. They may be obtained in shiny or satin finish and in indoor or outdoor grades.

Spray paints are not recommended, because they have too many disadvantages:

- They cover so sparingly that they require many coats in order to build up a solid color, or if you try to do it all at once, you have the problem of runs and drips.

- They are far more expensive than comparable non-spray products.

- Because of toxic fumes their use has to be restricted to adults and mature teenagers.

- Because of spray drift, a paint shield must be set up around the object being sprayed.

There has been much publicity recently about the harmful effects of aerosol sprays on the earth's protective layer of ozone which shields us from dangerous ultra-violet rays. This, however, is *not* among the disadvantages of clear plastic sprays and spray paints. The propellant implicated in the ozone depletion theory is fluorocarbon, which is used primarily for personal care products such as hair sprays and deodorants. The propellant used for paints, varnishes, and most household cleaners is hydrocarbon, which is not at the present time suspected of environmental damage.

BRUSHES

Using the right brush for a job can make any painting project easier, more fun, and better looking. Buy the best quality brushes available, or at least the best quality you can afford. And since you will only need one or two at most, they are not a major item of expense. One good brush will easily outlast two cheaper ones and give better results with less frustration.

To prolong the life of your brushes, and with care they will last much longer:

- Do not leave brushes standing on their bristles in jars of water or other solvent. They will bend out of shape quickly and will be almost impossible to get back in original shape.

   If you want to keep the bristle part in your water or solvent between color uses, suspend them so that the bristles are in the liquid but not touching the bottom of the container. To accomplish this, you can drill a small hole through your brush handle just above the metal ferrule and slip a piece of wire through the hole so that it rests on either edge of your container.

- Clean and wash brushes immediately after use. Even though acrylic paints are water soluble, if you let them dry hard in a brush you will never get the paint out and the brush is ruined.

- Keep brushes separated according to the solvent in which they are cleaned if you are using several different kinds of paint. Brushes that are cleaned with water, are best not interchanged with those cleaned with alcohol or turpentine.

The best brushes for use with pebble craft projects are:

Nylon brushes, which are always used for acrylic paints. They may be used for other paints too, of course. A flat brush is useful for covering large areas quickly, so a ½'' flat brush might be good to have. Also get at least one and perhaps two small, round, pointed brushes.

Soft bristle brushes (e.g., camel or squirrel hair) are useful for fine work, thin lines, or airplane enamels, where smoothness is essential. You can draw much finer lines with them than with nylon brushes. So get at least one small round one, about a number one or two size, for drawing those fine lines.

Brush substitutes are sometimes useful. Cotton swabs, or toothpicks can be used for small touch-ups, or when it's too much bother to clean a brush. A strip of cardboard or the plastic tab from a bread loaf wrapper can be used to apply a thin layer of contact cement. A sliver of wood can be used for the same purpose.

SOLVENTS

Solvents are used to thin paints and finishes and to clean brushes and fingers if necessary. The projects in this book all use acrylic paints or felt-tip markers, so the only solvent needed is water. However, should you decide to use other paints or varnishes in your experimenting, you may find this list helpful:

- *Denatured alcohol,* for shellac.

- *Turpentine,* for airplane enamels, oil paints, and polyurethane varnish.

- *Paint thinner* and *mineral spirits,* odorless, and equally effective, substitutes for turpentine.

- *Lacquer thinner,* for epoxy resin, polyester resin and contact cement.

Kerosene is a useful clean-up solvent to have around too. It's generally less expensive than turpentine and paint thinner but will work on most oil-based paints. It's useful for cleaning hands too.

PAPIER MACHÉ

This is a useful ancillary material if you want to smooth out the joints between your pebbles, or to add bumps to pebble where none exist naturally. You can of course make it up yourself by shredding newspaper and adding paste till you get a glutinous mass, but it's a tedious chore. It's much simpler and very inexpensive to get a small bag of the commercially prepared kind which lasts indefinitely and can be

180

mixed in any quantity simply by adding water. There are several different brands available and you might also use one of the prepared clays that set rock hard when dry. They just about all have the problem of shrinkage to a greater or lesser degree as the water content in them dries out. With a little experimentation, you'll find them easy to handle though.

BREAD DOUGH

There are many different recipes for bread dough for use in various crafts. Perhaps it's me, but I've had success with some and disasters with others. The simplest I have found for young children, and even old children come to that, is that made from packaged bread and white glue. The proportion is two slices of white sandwich bread with the crusts removed to one tablespoon of white glue. Break up the bread into small pieces, add the glue, and squish it all together until it turns into a compact dough. It's great for small additions like ears, noses, and assorted other small features on pebble creations.

KNIVES

Craft and utility knives make neater and more accurate cuts than scissors in most cases—particularly on cardboard and Styrofoam. They are also safer than razor blades. They usually consist of two parts, a handle and a retractable (or at least replaceable) blade. If you're going to buy one, look for one with the retractable feature—it's much safer to have lying around. *X-Acto* is a trade name for knives sold in hobby stores, which are narrow-handled and come with an assortment of blades. Hardware stores carry thick-handled knives with replaceable razor-like blades. Art stores carry mat-cutting knives which also have fat handles and razor-like blades. There is a very handy little knife with the trade name *Olfa*. It has a retractable, replaceable blade which is quite thin and

181

constructed so that the tip, when blunt, can be snapped off providing a new sharp working point thus providing twelve blades in one. Stanley knives have retractable blades and Lewis safety knives have an automatic blade guard. But with or without safety features, knives and razor blades should only be used by adults or mature teen-agers.

PROJECT INDEX

183

8768